Kansai Japanese

Learn the language as it is really spoken in Western Japan!

Curses and the macho style of male speech

Lover's language

Gangster, samurai, and other rough ways of speaking

Ōsaka, Hiroshima, and Kyōto Japanese

The polite haru style of Western Japanese speech

Men's and women's speech

Kansai Japanese

The Language of Ōsaka, Kyōto, and Western Japan

PETER TSE

CHARLES E. TUTTLE COMPANY
Rutland, Vermont & Tokyo, Japan

Published by the Charles E. Tuttle Company, Inc.
of Rutland, Vermont & Tokyo, Japan
with editorial offices at
2-6 Suido 1-chome, Bunkyo-ku, Tokyo 112

Library of Congress Catalog Card No. 92-061820
International Standard Book No. 0-8048-1868-1

First printing, 1993
Third printing, 1994

Printed in Japan

ACKNOWLEDGMENTS

I studied Western Japanese for several years without the help of a decent book in English on how people actually speak in Western Japan. If this book succeeds in filling that gap, it is only because many friends took the time to explain and speak Western Japanese to me. The ones who deserve most thanks are the ones who thought up and then checked the example sentences in this book. Special thanks go to Yae Kunida, Seigo Nakazawa, Yoshio Kurokawa, Shizuko Nakazawa, Noriko Marshall, Junko Omura, and my teacher Sakiko Ogo.

CONTENTS

FOREWORD

Are you living somewhere in the western half of Honshū? Like maybe Ōsaka, Kyōto, Kōbe, Okayama, Hiroshima, or just about anywhere west of Nagoya? Are you planning a visit to either the Kinki (Ōsaka-Kyōto-Nara-Kōbe) or Chūgoku (Okayama-Hiroshima-Shimonoseki) region? Do you want to understand the gangsters, geisha, and samurai who always appear in Japanese movies? You'll find, if it hasn't confused or maddened you already, that the everyday Japanese spoken in Western Japan is totally unlike the Japanese you have been studying. They understand your textbook Japanese just fine but you can't comprehend a word of what they say back to you; "they" meaning just about everybody speaking informally. They might be old people with all their stories to tell, your girlfriend or boyfriend, children, students in school uniforms, truck drivers, or just the regular people you meet at pubs, parties, or on the street. Think of all the listening practice you're missing by not understanding the real language spoken around you all the time.

If you really want to get to know Western Japan's people, you'll have to supplement your study of standard Japanese with Western Japanese. And with this book, you'll have all you need to understand what you're hearing in Western Japan and to communicate with friends, lovers, and foes in the language they really use.

KINKI AREA

Kyoto
Hyogo
KYOTO
Shiga
KOBE
Osaka
OSAKA
Mie
Nara
Wakayama
Sea of Japan
Pacific Ocean
HIROSHIMA
SHIMONOSEKI
TOKYO
OKAYAMA
N

1

AN INTRODUCTION TO KANSAI JAPANESE

The purpose of this book is to give you an in-depth and fun account of conversational Western Japanese. Hundreds of expressions are given first in Western Japanese, followed by Eastern Japanese and then English. Although this book is written primarily as a guide to Western Japanese, it can also be used to learn informal Japanese as spoken in Tōkyō, since all expressions are given in both Eastern and Western Japanese.

A WORD ABOUT REGIONAL NAMES

In this book, the term Western Japan describes the area of Honshū that is west of Nagoya. The Kinki district is an official geographical division that covers the prefectures of Shiga, Mie, Nara, Kyōto, Wakayama, Ōsaka, and Hyōgo. Kansai (literally, "west of the border") is more of a cultural and historical term loosely used to describe the core area around Kōbe, Ōsaka, and Kyōto. Chūgoku refers to the most western part of Honshū, where the cities Okayama, Hiroshima, and Shimonoseki are found.

The heart of Eastern Japan is Tōkyō. The term Kantō ("east of the border") is used to describe the greater Tōkyō region the way Kansai is used to describe the greater Ōsaka region.

WESTERN JAPANESE: A SHORT BACKGROUND

Western Japan has the longest history of all of Japan's regions.

Kinki and eastern Kyūshū are believed to be the areas of the country earliest settled by the Yamato people, ancestors of the present-day Japanese. The name Chūgoku, meaning "central country," shows that this region was once the center of ancient Japan. Kinki, moreover, was the capital region for over a thousand years, first with Nara from 600 to 794, and then with Kyōto from 794 to 1868.

Eastern Japanese became the national standard for modern Japan primarily because Tōkyō, then called Edo, was made the nation's capital in 1868. In fact, it seems that standard Japanese, or *hyōjungo,* was to some extent concocted from uptown Tōkyō and other dialects during the Meiji era to deal with the huge numbers of immigrants swarming into Tōkyō from all over Japan speaking mutually unintelligible dialects.

If by historical chance Western Japanese failed to become the modern standard for all of Japan, it still must be regarded as the standard language of western Honshū. Although *hyōjungo* has affected spoken Western Japanese in recent years thanks to mass communications and standardized schooling, Western Japanese will never be replaced by *hyōjungo* in Western Japan. Western Japanese has become the informal language of Western Japan, with *hyōjungo* reserved for formal occasions, news broadcasts, and the like.

There are many similar but distinct dialects within Western Japan itself. There's the crass sounding *Banshū-ben* spoken around Himeji on toward Okayama. There's the tough sounding *Ōsaka-ben,* and there's perhaps the most elegant sounding dialect in all Japan, refined *Kyōto-ben.* And this is just to name a few. Each dialect has its own special turns of phrase as well as unique slang and vocabulary. However, all western Honshū dialects are sufficiently alike to justify talking about a monolithic Western Japanese dialect. In this book emphasis is placed on the "standard" Western Japanese spoken by people in the central Kinki region. However, some attention is also paid to other versions of the dialect. There are short sections that focus on Hiroshima Japanese, polite Kyōto usage, and *Naniwa kotoba,* a certain style of Ōsaka Japanese spoken primarily by older people nowadays, but often heard on TV and radio in Ōsaka. These chapters should help listening skills considerably.

About The Format

Throughout this book, Western Japanese is contrasted with Eastern Japanese, which is the language of Tōkyō and surrounding areas. Eastern Japanese is not the same as *hyōjungo,* or standard Japanese, which is an ideal version of the language not flawlessly spoken by anyone except maybe newscasters and other professional talkers. Throughout this book, words and phrases given in Western Japanese are followed by the Eastern Japanese equivalent in meaning and tone. For instance, Ōsaka slang expressions are given in Tōkyō slang, not perfect *hyōjungo,* in order to preserve the right tone. An attempt is made to capture approximately the same tone in the English translations as well.

Each word or phrase is given first in Western Japanese (w), then in Eastern Japanese (e), and then in English. For example:

w: **A: Watashi Hawai ni iku tsumori ya.**
B: Honma ni?
e: *A: Watashi (wa) Hawai ni iku tsumori desu.*
B: Honto ni?
A: I plan to go to Hawaii.
B: Really?

Most words and phrases in this book will be understood throughout Western Japan. However, in some cases a word will be followed by the region's name, "(Hiroshima)" or "(Ōsaka)" for example, indicating that the word or phrase used is particular to that region.

PRONUNCIATION

The intonation of Western Japanese is said to be opposite that of Eastern Japanese. Whereas it's *"aME"* in Western Japanese, it's *"Ame"* in Eastern Japanese. Both mean rain. But if you use Tōkyō intonation and say *"Ame"* in Ōsaka it will mean candy, not rain. Similarly, there are characteristic pitch patterns within a sentence that set Western Japanese apart from most types of Eastern Japanese. For example, whereas it's "WATASHI WA AMERIKA-jin deSU" in Ōsaka, it's "Watashi WA aMErika-jin DEsu" in Tōkyō. In addition, there is a relative lack of crisp double consonants, such as *tt* or *kk,* in Western Japanese.

Although as immediately apparent to Japanese ears as an English accent is to American ears, the difference in intonation between Western and Eastern Japanese is generally too subtle for English speakers to hear or imitate without having lived in Japan for a period of time. Unless you are a linguistic genius or under the age of six, you will probably end up speaking Japanese with a foreign accent anyway, so this book leaves the differences in Western Japanese intonation aside and concentrates on the differences in wording. If there is any pitch pattern you should imitate, it is that of newscasters, since their intonation has the greatest legitimacy.

MEN'S AND WOMEN'S KANSAI TALK

Men and women tend to speak more alike in Western Japan than they do in Kantō. For example, the particle *na* will generally be replaced by *ne* in women's speech in Eastern Japan. However, in Western Japan it is not at all uncommon to hear women say *na,* especially when talking informally. Similarly, the particle *wa* used for feminine emphasis in Eastern Japanese is often used by men in Western Japan. It is common for men to say *Hayō ikana akan wa* (I have to go right away) in Western Japan, with the *wa* lending emphasis, not femininity, to the sentence.

Although most words and phrases in this book can be used by either sex, women tend to avoid particularly rough or vulgar sounding talk, and men tend to avoid effeminate sounding talk. The ♀ and ♂ symbols are used to point out those words and phrases that should not be used by the opposite sex.

As you probably know, men and women use different pronouns in Japanese. However, in order to save space, if a sentence as said by men and women only differs in pronouns, ♂ or ♀ is not indicated. With the help of the pronoun chart that follows, it is easy to switch from women's talk to men's talk and vice versa. This is especially so with Western Japanese, where differences between male and female speech are less marked than in Eastern Japanese.

The many pronouns for "I," "you," and "he" in Japanese carry a range of nuances not found in English. However, pronouns are omitted completely when the meaning is clear from the context. Bear in mind that Japanese speakers avoid pronouns for "you," "he," or "she" whenever a title or name can be used instead.

Men's Pronouns

Boku (I, cordial or friendly)
Bokura, Bokutachi (We)
Ore (I, tough, atmosphere of comradery or intimacy)
Orera, Oira (We)
Washi, Wate (I, senior or patronizing, common in Western Japan)
Watashi (I, neutral, polite)
Watashidomo, Watashitachi (We)
Watakushi (I, very formal)
Watakushidomo (We, very formal)
Wagahai or *Yo* (I, for noblemen, archaic, heard in samurai movies)
Ware (I, for commoners, archaic, heard in samurai movies)

Wareware (We, modern, polite, but abstract as in "we Japanese")

Temē, Kisama (You, Eastern Japan, vulgar, said when fighting or insulting someone)

Ware (You, Western Japan, like *"temē"*, used by gangsters, etc., to intimidate)

Omae, Omē (You, tough, intimate or insulting)

Omaera (You all, tough, intimate or insulting)

Kimi (You, cordial or patronizing, not common in Western Japan, heard often in songs)

Anata (You, polite)

Anatatachi, Anatagata (You all)

Aitsu, Yatsu (He, tough, familiar, used by men to refer to men)

Koitsu (He, She, or You, meaning "the (in view) scoundrel")

Soitsu (He or She, meaning "that guy")

Ano hito (He or She, polite)

Ano kata (He or She, very polite)

Kare (He, polite, distant, not used for friends)

Karera (They, polite)

Kanojo (She, polite, distant, not used for friends)

Women's Pronouns

Atashi (I, affectedly feminine)

Atashitachi (We, affectedly feminine)

Watashi (I, polite, most commonly used pronoun)

Watakushi (I, very formal)

Warawa (I, archaic, heard in samurai movies)

Anta (You, common in Western Japan, intimate or somewhat mothering, sometimes also used by men)

Anata (You, polite, a wife to her husband meaning "dear" or "darling")

Boku (You, to little boys who call themselves *boku*)

Ano hito, Ano kata, Kare, Kanojo (same as Men's above)

A Little Advice

Although speaking Western Japanese to your friends in Ōsaka, Kyōto, or Kōbe will allow you to get closer to them, speaking Western Japanese in Tōkyō might seem as outlandish as hearing a Japanese exchange student back home speaking jive or cockney. On the other hand, speaking only perfect *hyōjungo* in informal situations in Western Japan would be like speaking perfect BBC English in casual occasions back home. Just like you do in English, you should adapt your style of speech to the situation and the person you are speaking to. In any case, your Japanese friends in Western Japan will absolutely love to hear you speak their dialect.

In order to become really good in a foreign language, you have to live it. Study is important, but to become fluent in Japanese you must do everything in Japanese: eating, socializing, playing sports, and working. While this is not always possible, you can at least insist on speaking Japanese to Japanese, especially to the many people who assault you with their English the second they hear you speaking Japanese with an accent. In order to avoid this, even as a beginner, you can and should say a number of things. Be polite but clear. They are the ones being inconsiderate.

Sumimasen ga, watashi wa Eigo wakarimasen.
Excuse me, I don't speak English.

Nihongo de hanashite kudasai.
Please speak Japanese.

Nihongo de hanashite ii desu ka?
Can we speak Japanese please?

Nihongo o benkyō suru tame ni Nihon ni irun desu kara, nihongo de hanashitain desu ga.
I'm in Japan to study Japanese, so I'd like to speak Japanese.

When you don't understand something, don't give up! Try to control the pace of the conversation with phrases like:

Mō chotto yukkuri hanashite kudasai.
Please speak a bit slower.

Mō ichido itte kudasai.
Please say that again.

Nan 'tte?
What was that?

Setsumei shinaoshite kuremasu ka?
Could you explain that a different way?

SEVEN MAJOR DIFFERENCES BETWEEN WESTERN AND EASTERN JAPANESE

Broadly speaking, the main differences between Western and Eastern Japanese can be summarized in seven points.

1. Verbal negatives end in *nai* in Eastern Japanese but in *hen* (primarily Kansai) or *n* (primarily Chūgoku) in Western Japanese.

	Eastern Japanese	Western Japanese
doesn't eat	*tabenai*	*tabehen, taben*
doesn't know	*shiranai*	*shirahen, shiran*
doesn't think	*omowanai*	*omowahen, omowan*
doesn't write	*kakanai*	*kakahen, kakehen, kakan*
doesn't come	*konai*	*kēhen, kon*
doesn't do	*shinai*	*sēhen, sen*
isn't, aren't	*nai*	*arahen, arehen*
isn't doing	*yattenai*	*yattehen*
can't do	*dekinai*	*dekehen, dekihin*
can't write	*kakenai*	*kakehen, kakarehen*

Moreover, the polite *-masen* ending of Eastern Japanese negative verbs becomes *-mahen* in Western Japanese.

	Eastern Japanese	Western Japanese
doesn't eat	*tabemasen*	*tabemahen*
doesn't go	*ikimasen*	*ikimahen*
excuse me	*suimasen*	*sunmahen*

2. The past tense of verbal negatives ends in *-nakatta* in Eastern Japanese and in *-henkatta* or *-nkatta* in Western Japanese.

	Eastern Japanese	Western Japanese
didn't eat	*tabenakatta*	*tabehenkatta, tabenkatta*
didn't know	*shiranakatta*	*shirankatta*
didn't think	*omowanakatta*	*omowahenkatta, omowankatta*
didn't do	*yaranakatta*	*yarehenkatta*
wasn't doing	*yattenakatta*	*yattehenkatta*

3. The past tense of Eastern Japanese verbs has a double "tt" sound, but Western Japanese frequently has a single "t" sound instead, sometimes accompanied by a long vowel sound like "ō." Eastern Japanese, unlike Western Japanese, accentuates crisp double consonants.

	Eastern Japanese	Western Japanese
thought	*omotta*	*omōta, omota*
received	*moratta*	*morōta, morota*
made a mistake	*machigatta*	*machigōta*
finished up	*shimatta*	*shimōta, shimota*
bought	*katta*	*kōta*
bought	*katte shimatta*	*kōte shimōta*
said	*itta*	*yūta, yutta*
used	*tsukatta*	*tsukōta, tsukota*
met	*atta*	*ōta*

4. The verb "to be" for animals and people is *iru* in Eastern Japanese and *oru* in Western Japanese.

	Eastern Japanese	Western Japanese
is	*iru*	*oru*
isn't	*inai*	*orahen, orehen, oran*
wasn't	*inakatta*	*orehenkatta, orankatta*
was	*ita*	*otta*
isn't being	*itenai, inai*	*ottehen, orahen*
wasn't being	*itenakatta, inakatta*	*ottehenkatta, orahenkatta*

5. The copula *da* of Eastern Japanese is *ya* (primarily Kansai) or *ja* (primarily Chūgoku) in Western Japanese. Although not strictly equivalent, these words can be thought of as functioning like the verb "to be."

	Eastern Japanese	Western Japanese
is	*da*	*ya, ja*
was	*datta*	*yatta, jatta*
likely is	*darō*	*yarō, yaro, jarō, jaro*

6. The adverbial form of adjectives ends in *ku* in Eastern Japanese, but usually lacks *ku* in Western Japanese. Instead of *ku,* both single and double vowel sounds are commonly heard.

	Eastern Japanese	Western Japanese
become hot	*atsuku naru*	*atsū naru, atsu naru*
eat fast	*hayaku taberu*	*hayō taberu, hayo taberu*
understand well	*yoku wakaru*	*yō wakaru*
kindly, well	*yoroshiku*	*yoroshū*
busily and . . .	*isogashikute*	*isogashiite, isogashūte*

7. The imperative form of verbs in Western Japanese can differ from Eastern Japanese. Both forms, however, are commonly used in Western Japan.

	Eastern Japanese	Western Japanese
eat fast!	*hayaku tabero!*	*hayō tabē! hayo tabe!*
wake up!	*okiro!*	*okii ya! oki!*
go!	*ike!*	*ikii! iki!*
read!	*yome!*	*yomii! yomē!*
study!	*benkyō shiro!*	*benkyō shii! benkyō shii ya!*

2

STANDARD KANSAI LANGUAGE

While old people in Kyōto, Kōbe, Nagoya, Ōsaka, Okayama, and Hiroshima speak noticeably distinct strains of Western Japanese, there seems to be a trend toward a new standard for the region. The basis for this standard is the speech of the Kyōto-Kōbe-Ōsaka region. Although differences exist from speaker to speaker and from locale to locale, in the degree to which the local dialect and Tōkyō expressions have been incorporated, most of what the younger generation says in Western Japan will match the Japanese in this chapter. In later chapters the traditional styles of Kyōto, Ōsaka, and Hiroshima speech, now mostly spoken by rural and older people, will be covered in depth.

HOW MUCH?

If you go to one of Kyōto's many temple flea markets, such as the one at Kitano-Tenmangu on the 25th of each month, you're bound to hear some tough bargaining. These markets are good for finding traditional wares and food, and great for hearing Western Japanese in action.

w: **Kore nanbo ya?**
e: *Kore wa ikura desu ka?*
How much is this?

w: **Mittsu kōtara chotto makete kurehen ka?**

e: *Mittsu kattara chotto makete kuremasen ka?*
If I buy three will you lower the price a little?

w/e: ***Hai, hassen en ni maketokō.***
O.K. I'll lower it to eight thousand yen.

w: **A: Chotto maketoite ya.**
B: Sunmahen, makarimahen nen.
e: *A: Sukoshi waribiki dekimasen ka?*
B: Gomen nasai, waribiki dekinain desu.
A: Can you reduce the price a little?
B: Sorry, I can't give a discount.

w: **Oterasan no nominoichi wa doko?**
e: *Otera no nominoichi wa doko?*
Where's the temple flea market?

People in Kansai affix *san* to certain words. They refer to temples as *oterasan.* Older people say *arigatosan* (thank you), *ohayōsan* (good morning), *eraisan* (big shot), and *ansan* (polite you).

w: **Kore wa bottakuri yatta.**
e: *Kau kachi wa nakatta./Borareta.*
This was a rip-off.

Bottakuru means to overcharge.

w: **Kore wa honma ni horidashimon ya.**
e: *Kore wa honto ni horidashimono da.*
This is a real bargain.

w: **Machigainō ureru.**
e: *Machigainaku ureru.*
You'll have no problem selling these.

Nambo can also be substituted for other meanings of *ikura.*

w: **Nanbo yattemo wakarahen wa!**
e: *Ikura yattemo wakaranai yo!*
No matter how many times I try to do it, I still don't understand!

w: **Nanbo demo motte kite.**
e: *Ikura demo motte kite kudasai.*
Bring as many as you feel like.

w: **Nanbo nandemo aisu kuriimu gurai kōte kuretemo ēn chau?**
e: *Ikura nandemo aisu kuriimu gurai katte kuretemo iin ja nai?*
Don't you think that you could at least buy some ice cream for me?

w: **Nanbo nandemo sore wa hidoi wa.**
e: *Ikura nandemo sore wa hidoi desu.*
That's absolutely horrible.

GREETINGS

If you walk into a little mom-and-pop shop around Kyōto, you'll probably be greeted with *oideyasu* rather than the standard *irasshai.* And when you leave you will probably hear *maido* or *ōkini* rather than the standard *arigatō gozaimasu.*

w: **Maido, ōkini!**
e: *Domo arigatō gozaimasu!*
Thank you very much!

Maido literally means "every time," but carries the nuance of "always at your service." *Ōkini* means "thank you," and sounds friendlier than *arigatō gozaimasu.*

w: **Oideyasu!/Yō okoshi!/Okoshiyasu!**
e: *Irasshai!*
Come in! Welcome!

w: **Gomenyasu.**
e: *Gomen kudasai.*
Anybody home?/Sorry to trouble you.

This is said, for example, when you are calling in the front door in hopes that somebody is in.

w: **Hisashiburi ya ne.**
e: *Hisashiburi desu ne.*
Long time no see.

w: **Ē tenki ya ne.**
e: *Ii tenki desu ne.*
Nice day, isn't it.

The expressive particles *na* and *ne* can be used interchangeably. *Na* sounds a lot tougher than *ne,* and its use is frowned upon by delicate people. Be that as it may, both men and women use *na* all the time in Western Japan, much more so than in Tōkyō.

w: **Sunmahen. /Sunmasen.**
e: *Sumimasen./Suimasen.*
Excuse me.

Sunmahen is not considered to be as polite as *sumimasen.* It is very effective, however, when you need people out of the way in a hurry, like when you are trying to shove your way out of a packed train.

Os, Ya, and *Oi* are common informal greetings in both Western and Eastern Japanese. *Os* has a tough air of comradery. It is used among teammates and the like, although teenage girls also use it. *Ya* would be used, for example, when some people see their colleagues sitting at another table in a pub. *Konban wa* would sound too formal in such a situation. *Oi* would be used when you see a kid stealing your bike across the street.

w/e: ***Konnichiwa. /Konbanwa.***
Good day./Good evening.

w: **Ohayō./Ohayōsan dosu.**
e: *Ohayō gozaimasu.*
Good morning.

w/e: ***Oyasumi. /Oyasuminasai.***
Good night.

HOW ARE YOU?

Like people the world over, the Japanese exchange greetings with people they know. However, unlike Americans, Japanese rarely say hello to people they pass on the street unless they have actually met them.

w: **Genki ka?**
e: *Genki?*
Feeling good?

w/e: ***Mm! Genki yo!***
Yeah, I'm feeling great!

w: **Genki ya.**
e: *Genki da yo.*
I'm fine.

w: **Nanka kawatta koto atta ka?**
e: *Nanika kawatta koto atta?*
Anything new happened recently?

w: **Nanka attan ka?/Nanka attan chau?**
e: *Nanika atta no?*
Is something the matter?

w/e: ***Betsu ni (nani mo).***
Nothing's wrong.

w/e: ***Betsu ni nan demo nai.***
Nothing in particular (is bothering me).

w: **Betsu ni kamahen.**
e: *Betsu ni kamawanai.*
I don't care./O.K. whatever.

w/e: ***Ma./Mā ne./Mā na.***
Nothing worth mentioning.

w: **Donai shitotten?** ♂/ **Donai shitetan?**
e: *Dō shiteta?*
How've you been?

w: **Aitsu donai shiten nen?** ♂/**Ano ko dōshiten no?** ♀
e: *Dō shiten dai?* ♂/*Aitsu (ano hito, kare) dō shiteru?*
How's he doing?

w: **Do shitan?/Nanka attan?**
e: *Dō shitan da?* ♂/*Dō shita no?*
What's the matter?

w: **Nani yattottan?/Nani yattotten?**
e: *Nani yatteta?*
What were you doing?/What have you been doing?

w: **Nani hanashitotten?/Nani hanashitottan?**
e: *Nani o hanashiteta no?*
What were you talking about?/ What have you been talking about?

w: **Daijōbu ya.**
e: *Daijōbu da.*
It's fine.

REALLY?!

One of the most common words in everyday Japanese is *honto,* or in Western Japanese, *honma.*

w: **Honma?**

e: *Honto?/Hontō?*
Really?

w: **Honma ni sō ya na.**
e: *Honto ni sō da ne.*
That's really the way it is.

w/e: ***Sono tōri.***
What you're saying is absolutely right.

w: **Honmakaina!**
e: *Honto ka yo!* ♂/*Uso!*
You gotta be kidding./You can't be for real.

w: **Sonna koto arukaina.**
e: *Sonna koto aru ka yo.* ♂/*Sonna koto aru hazu (wa) nai.*
It can't exist./It can't be there./He can't possibly have it.

w: **Kyōryū ga ottakaina.**
e: *Kyōryū ga ita ka yo.* ♂/*Kyōryū ga ita hazu wa nai.*
Dinosaurs can't possibly have existed.

w: **Chotto sakki koko wa doko kaina 'te kanji yatta.**
e: *Chotto mae koko wa doko ka na to iu kanji datta ne.*
Just a second ago I had a feeling like I didn't know where in the world I was.

The expression *-kaina,* which means "it can't be so," should not be confused with the male question mark *kai. Kai* is not used much in Western Japan.

w: **Nanka hen ka?** ♂/**Nanka hen?**
e: *Nanka okashii no kai?* ♂
Is something weird?

w: **Honma kamo na./Honma kamo wakarehen na./Honma kamo shirehen./Honma kamo shiren.**
e: *Honto kamo ne./Honto kamo wakaranai ne.*
Maybe it's really true.

w: **Sō ieba sō ya na.**
e: *Sō ieba sō desu ne.*
It hadn't occurred to me, but you're right.

w: **Sō ya de!**
e: *Sō da yo!*
It's like I say!

w: **Sō ya na.**
e: *Sō desu ne.*
That's so./I agree (with what you're saying).

w: **Sora sō ya.**
e: *Sore wa sō da.*
That's for sure.

w: **Atarimae yanka./Atarimae yan. /Atarimae ya.**
e: *Atarimae (da yo).*
It's obvious.
It makes sense.

w: **Ēn chau ka?**
e: *Iin ja nai ka?*
It's good, isn't it?

w: **Ē nā.**
e: *Ii nā.*
I'm envious.
That's great.

w: **Yute mi.**
e: *Itte mite.*
Try to say it.

w: **Sora waya ya na!/Sora waya kucha ya na!**
e: *Sore wa mecha da ne!*
That's out of control!

w: **Mō waya ya.**
e: *Mō mecha mecha da.*
It's already turned bad.

Waya in Western Japanese and *mecha* in Eastern Japanese are expressions used to describe situations that have become chaotic or totally out of control.

w: **Nande?/Nande ya nen?/Nande ya?**
e: *Dōshite?*
Why?

w: **Nande yarō?**
e: *Dōshite darō?*
What for?/What on earth?

w: **Sō nan?/Sō?**
e: *Sō nano?/Sō?*
Is that right?

w/e: ***Sokka./Sōkka./Naruhodo.***
Is that so./I see.

Although *a so desu ka?* also means "is that so?" it is rarely used among friends because it sounds stuffy and formal. *Sokka* and *naruhodo* are much more casual.

w: **Sora dō demo ē kedo . . .**
e: *Betsu ni iin dakedo . . .*
Anyway . . ./At any rate . . .

w: **Dotchi demo ē.**
e: *Nan demo ii.*
Whatever./Either's fine.

FOOD AND DRINK

In Western Japan, men refer to women in a friendly way as *onēchan* (big sister) if they don't know them. Likewise, women refer to men as *oniichan* (big brother) even if the man is younger.

w: **Onēchan, biiru ippon moraemakka? (Ōsaka)**
e: *Sumimasen, biiru ippon.*
Can I have a bottle of beer, please?

w: **Biiru ippon chōdai.**
e: *Biiru ippon kudasai.*
One bottle of beer, please.

Chōdai sounds more familiar than *kudasai* and is used, for example, by regular customers. It is also used in Eastern Japan, but not quite as frequently. Checkout clerks say *ni-hyaku-en chōdai itashimasu,* which means "two hundred yen, please."

w: **Kore chūkaryōri (to) chau yaro.**
e: *Kore wa chūkaryōri ja nai deshō.*
I'm pretty sure this isn't Chinese food.

w: **Gottsuosan (deshita).**
e: *Gochisōsama (deshita).*
Thanks for the great meal.

w: **Chotto otchan, kashiwa ōmori ni shitoite ne.**
e: *Chotto ojisan, toriniku ōmori ni shitoite ne.*
Please give me a lot of chicken, (Uncle).

Kashiwa is Kansai slang for chicken; in Tōkyō it means "oak tree." The above sentence might be said at a marketplace. *Otchan* is a friendly abbreviation of *ojichan,* literally "uncle." In Japan it is not considered rude to call a shop clerk *obasan* (aunt) or *ojisan* (uncle).

w: **Mō tabete shimōtan ya. /Mō tabete mōta.**
e: *Mō tabechatta.*
I already ate.

w: **Mō tabetan yarō.**
e: *Mō tabetan darō.*
They probably already ate.

In most cases *yarō* can be replaced with *yaro,* just as *darō* can be replaced with *daro.* If the above sentences were said with a rising intonation, they would become questions meaning "You ate already, didn't you?" The question-mark particle *ka* is generally omitted, although this is more common in Western Japanese.

w: **Tabetemo kamahen?/Tabetemo kamahen ka?**
e: *Tabetemo kamaimasen?/Tabetemo kamawanai?*
Do you mind if I eat?

w: **Aitsu meshi motte kaette kureru nente.** ♂
e: *Aitsu meshi o motte kaette kureru 'te.* ♂
He said he'd bring food back for us.

w: **Nanka mono-taran wa./Nanka mono-tarahen wa.**
e: *Nanika mono-taranai./Nanika mono-tarinai.*
This meal was somehow incomplete.

The previous sentence is said before suggesting that everybody go and have ice cream or something after a meal.

w: **Oishii (wa)!**
e: *Oishii (ne)!*
It's delicious!

w: **Mazui wa!/Mazu!**
e: *Mazui!*
It tastes awful!

Mazui can also be used to refer to rotten behavior, like when a friend double-crosses you.

w: **Nurukute ē nen.**
e: *Nurukute mo ii.*
It's O.K. if it's lukewarm.

w: **Nonde mi.**
e: *Nonde mite.*
Try a sip.

w: **Tabete mi.**
e: *Tabete mite.*
Try a bite.

w: **Ocha ni iko ka?**
e: *Kissaten ni ikō ka?*
Let's go to a coffee shop.

w/e: ***Hara hetta. Meshi kuwase!*** (rude command)
I'm hungry. Feed me a meal!

The usual way to say "I'm hungry" is *onaka suita. Hara hetta* is a tough-sounding alternative. *Meshi* is rather coarse slang for *gohan* (rice or food). *Kuwase* comes from the verb *kuu,* which sounds rougher than *taberu,* although both mean "to eat."

w: **Obachan no okonomiyaki wa oishi omanna.**
e: *Koko no okonomiyaki wa saikō desu ne.*
Your okonomiyaki is superb.

Okonomiyaki, a speciality of Western Japan, is a kind of pancake made from eggs, flour, shredded cabbage, ginger, and toppings, such as fish flakes, powdered seaweed, and sauce. Hiroshima's *okonomiyaki* is very big with lots of extras and is possibly the most delicious in Japan. Ōsaka's is great too. Tōkyō's *okonomiyaki* has a reputation for being small and bland.

THAT'S WRONG!

Chau is not Italian for goodbye. Nor is it a breed of dog. It is not even a word for Japanese food. *Chau* is an abbreviation of *chigau,* and is one of the most frequently used words in Western Japanese.

w: **Chau de.**
e: *Chigau yo.* ♂
That's wrong.

w: **Chaun (to) chau?**
e: *Chigaun ja nai?*
That's wrong, isn't it?

w: **Chau chau.**
e: *Chigau chigau.*
That's wrong.

w: **Chau wa.**

e: *Chigau.*
Wait, I'm mistaken.

This is said after you realize you've just said something wrong.

w: **Zenzen chaimasu yo!/Zenzen chau de!**
e: *Zenzen chigau yo!*
That's completely wrong!

w: **Nanka chigaun ka?/Nanka chaun ka?/Nanka chau no?**
e: *Nanka chigau no?*
Is something wrong?/Something's not right?

w: **Uso yarō!**
e: *Uso darō!*
That's a lie!/No way!

w/e: ***Uso bakkari./Uso tsuki.***
Liar!

w: **Akan de./Akan wa./Muri ya de.**
e: *Muri da yo.*
That's impossible.

w: **A: Ashita eiga ni ikeru?**
B: Akan wa. Ikarehen.
e: *A: Ashita eiga ni ikeru?*
B: Muri da. Ikenai yo.
A: Can you go to the movies tomorrow?
B: No way. I can't go.

w: **Muda ya yū no yatto wakatten na.**
e: *Muda da to iu koto yatto wakatta ne./ . . . wakattan da ne.*
You finally realize that it's a waste.

A "waste of time" is *jikan no muda.* A "waste of money" is *okane no muda.* Some speakers abbreviate *to iu koto* to just *iu koto.*

w: **(To) yū koto wa ikan yaro.**
e: *(To) iu koto wa ikanain daro.*
That is, he probably won't go.

Another way to say "that is" or "in other words" is *tsumari.*

w: **Yūtara akan zo.** ♂
e: *Ittara dame da zo.* ♂
Don't say it./Don't tell him.

w: **Nani yatten ne ya!/Nani yatten nen!**
e: *Nani yatteru!/Nani yatten da!* ♂
Hey, what are you doing!

w: **Nani kangaeton ya, aho!**
e: *Nani kangaeten daro, baka!*
What are you thinking, you fool!

w: **Sonna aho na.**
e: *Sonna baka na.*
I've never seen (heard) such a stupid thing in all my life.

w: **Yō yū wa!**
e: *Yoku iu yo!*
You're full of it!

This is said jokingly to someone who is making false claims.

w: **Mō ē.**
e: *Mō ii.*
That's enough.

w: **Mō ē wa!**
e: *Mō iin da yo!*
Enough already!

w: **Makashi.**
e: *Makasenasai.*
Leave it to me. /Trust me.

w: **Dekihin./Dekehen.**
e: *Dekinai.*
I can't do it.

FEELING SICK

If you get a sty in your eye in Western Japan, you get *mebachiko.* But if you come down with the same ailment in Tōkyō, you get *monomorai.* Just to confuse you, *monomorai* means "beggar" in Kansai. So when in Kansai, if you don't want a beggar in your eye, you had better say *mebachiko.*

w: **Mebachiko ga dekita.**
e: *Monomorai ga dekita.*
I have a sty in my eye.

w: **Kaze hikan yō ni, bōshi kabutta hō ga ē.**
e: *Kaze hikanai tame ni, bōshi kabutta hō ga ii yo.*
You'd better put on a hat so you won't get sick.

w: **Sonna shimpai sende (mo) ē yan. /Sonnan (wa) shimpai sende ē yo.**
e: *Sonna shimpai iranai yo.*
You don't need to worry about it./Stop worrying.

w: **Bochi bochi ya na./Bochi bochi denna. (Ōsaka)**

e: *Ma ma desu ne.*
You know, so so.

w: **Aitsu nanka funya funya shiten na. / Aitsu nanka funya funya shiton na.** ♂
e: *Aitsu nanka funya funya shiteru ne.*
He was flopping around like he had no bones.

w: **Mō akite shimōta. /Mō akite mōta. /Mō aki ga kita.**
e: *Mō akichatta.*
I'm sick of it already./I've had enough already.

A more vehement way of saying this is *unzari shita,* meaning "I've had it up to here!"

w: **Ano hito mō shinde (shi)mōtan ya te.**
e: *Ano hito mō shinjatta 'te.*
I heard he already died.

w: **Mō isogashūte isogashūte me ga mawaru.**
e: *Mō isogashikute isogashikute me ga mawaru.*
I'm so busy I'm going crazy.

w: **Nanka hakisō ya.**
e: *Nanka hakisō da.*
I feel like I'm going to throw up./He looks like he's going to throw up.

w: **Nanka muka muka suru wa.**
e: *Chotto muka muka shiteru wa.*
I feel a little nauseous.

w: **Onara shitan wa dare yarō!**
e: *Onara shita no (wa) dare?*
O.K. Who farted?

w: **Onara sentoite! Mō!/Onara sentoki! Mō!**
e: *Onara shinaide! Mō!/Onara suru na!* ♂
Stop farting already!

Sentoki is the command form of *sentoite.* The Eastern Japanese command form *suru na* sounds even stronger than the Western Japanese command.

w: **Ano hito nanka shinikake mitai ya.**
e: *Ano hito nanka shinikaketeru yō da.*
That man looks like he's about to die.

Not Aware

In Japanese *bōtto* is not a ship, it's a state of mind, or perhaps lack of a state of mind. In English it is what we commonly call "spacing out."

w: **Itsumo bōtto shitetara, atama ga dandan sabite shimaun ya.**
e: *Itsumo bōtto shitetara, atama ga dandan sabite shimau.*
If you space out all the time, you'll gradually go senile.

w: **Ippen mō yūta kedo, wakarehenkatta yarō.**
e: *Ikkai mō itta kedo, wakaranakatta darō.*
I told him once already, but he probably didn't understand.

w: **Wakarimahen./Wakarahen./ Wakarehen ./Wakaran.**
e: *Wakarimasen./Wakaranai./Wakannai.*
I don't understand.

w: **Gomen, machigōta.**
e: *Gomen, machigatta.*
Sorry, I made a mistake.

w: **Wakarehen sonnan!/Sonnan wakaran yan!**
e: *Wakaranai sonna!*
How am I supposed to know that?

The *n* at the end of *sonnan,* an abbreviation of *sonna no,* is more like the nasal "n" of "-ing" without the "g" sound. *Yan* and *ya* are similar in meaning, but not always interchangeable. *Yan* is harsher than *ya.*

w: **Yō wakarehen kedo . . .**
e: *Yoku wakaranain da kedo . . .*
I'm not sure but . . .

w: **Wakaru wake nai yan.**
e: *Wakaru wake nai.*
There's no way of knowing.

w: **Sō omowahen ka?/Sō omoehen ka?**
e: *Sō omowanai?*
Don't you think so?

w: **Shirahen sore wa./Shiran.**
e: *Shiranai sore wa.*
I don't know.

w: **Zenzen wakarahen.**
e: *Zenzen wakannai./Zenzen wakaranai.*
I don't understand at all.

w: **Nan nimo yuwahen kamo shirehen nen.**
e: *Nani mo iwanai kamo shirenai.*
He might say nothing.

w: **Nantomo yuwarehen nen./Nantomo ien na./Nantomo yuwen na.**
e: *Nantomo ienai.*
I have nothing to say about it.

w: **Nande?/Nande ya?/Nande ya nen?**
e: *Dōshite?/Nande?*
Why?

w: **Dō iu imi?** (polite)
e: *Dō iu imi deshō ka? (polite)*
What do you mean?

w: **Ittai sore wa dō iu imi ya nen?**
e: *Ittai sore wa dō iu imi da yo?*
What on earth do you mean?

w: **Kirai ya yūteta noni nande ittan?**

e: *Kirai datte itteta noni dōshite itta no?*
You said you hated it, yet you still went. How come?

w: **Nande akan nen?**
e: *Dōshite dame desu ka?*
What's wrong with it?

FAMILY TALK

There is one aspect of family talk that is the same throughout Japan, namely the greetings for coming and going. When coming home, members say *tadaima* and the whole family chimes in with *okaerinasai* or *okaeri,* meaning "welcome back home." When leaving, it's *itte kimasu* or *itte kuru,* which means "I'm going (but will be back later)," and gets a response of *itterasshai,* or "see you later." *Sayonara* is rarely used between family members unless parting for a long time. *Sayonara* and other expressions for "goodbye" have been virtually replaced in young people's speech with *bai bai.*

w: **Kane arahen kara harawarehen/ . . . harawaren.**
e: *Okane nai kara hararenai.*
I don't have money so I can't pay.

w: **Nanmo kōtehen.**
e: *Nanimo kattenai.*
He hasn't bought anything.

w: **Omutsu yara fuku yara kōta.**
e: *Oshime ya fuku katta.*
I bought diapers and clothes and things.

w: **A: Mō hayo ne!**
B: Se ya kedo motto okitokitai nen mon!

e: *A: Hayaku nenasai!*
B: Datte motto okitokitain da mon!
A: Go straight to bed!
B: But c'mon, I want to stay up longer!

w: **Naru yō ni naru yan.**
e: *Naru yō ni naru sa.*
What will be will be.

w: **Anta gokuraku tombo ya ne.**
e: *Anata kiraku ne.*
You like the good life, don't you.

A *gokuraku tombo,* literally "dragonfly of paradise," is a person who doesn't worry about anything, is kind of lazy, drifts, has no drive, and yet loves luxury and good food whether he has the money or not. He is the opposite of a *hatarakimono,* a conscientious hard-worker, but has certain qualities in common with a *namakemono,* a lazy-bones.

w: **Daremo kiitehen.**
e: *Daremo kiitenai.*
Nobody's listening.

w: **Gomi o hotte kurehen ka?/Gomi o hokashite kurehen ka?**
e: *Gomi o sutete kurenai?*
Won't you throw out the garbage (for me)?

Horu or *hokasu* means "to throw out" in Western Japanese. This would not be understood in Tōkyō.

w: **Ojiichan mukashi kono dōgu tsukōtotta.**
e: *Ojiichan mukashi kono dōgu o tsukatteta.*
Grandpa once used this tool.

w: **Tsukue no ue naoshite.**
e: *Tsukue no ue katashite./Tsukue no ue katazukete.*
Please clean up the stuff on the desk.

Naosu means "to fix" or "to heal someone." In Western Japanese, it has the additional meaning of cleaning up in the sense of putting things in order. Cleaning up in the sense of vacuuming is *sōji suru.*

w: **Anta yattetan chau ka?**
e: *Anata yattetan ja nai?*
You did it, right?

w: **Nanmo nai. /Nanmo arehen nen.**
e: *Nanimo nai.*
I have nothing./There's nothing.

w: **O-mizu (o) machigōta sakai (ni) gohan ga yawarakasugiru.**
e: *O-mizu (o) machigaeta kara gohan ga yawarakasugiru.*
I made a mistake with the water, so the rice is too soft.

Sakai ni is "because" or "therefore" in Western Japanese.

w: **Aitsu ga shigoto yameyotta. /Watashi (wa) shigoto yameta.**
e: *Aitsu ga shigoto yameta./Watashi (wa) shigoto yameta.*
He quit his job./I quit my job.

The verb-ending *-yotta* or *-yōta* is rather coarse and is used to refer to people other than oneself. It adds emphasis with the nuance that the outcome was either unexpected or undesirable. There is no equivalent in Eastern Japanese.

w: **Sono toki shigoto yametotta.**

e: *Sono toki shigoto yameteta.*
I had quit my job at that time.

w: **Ano hito yatto chōjō o kiwameyotta.**
e: *Aitsu yatto chōjō kiwameta.*
He's finally reached the top.

w: **Minna mō dete itte shimōta(n ya).**
e: *Minna mō dete itchatta.*
Everybody has left already.

w: **Itsumo tsuri ni ittoru noni zenzen tsurehen.**
e: *Itsumo tsuri ni itteru noni zenzen tsurenai.*
Even though he always goes fishing, he never catches anything.

w: **Nande naitotta (okottotta)?**
e: *Doshite naiteta (okotteta)?*
Why were you crying (angry)?

w: **Mukō ni otta kedo, doko ni itta ka na?**
e: *Mukō ni ita kedo, doko ni itta no ka na?*
He was there, but I wonder where he went?

w: **Hayō ne ni ikii ya!**
e: *Hayaku ne ni ikinasai!/Hayaku ne ni ike!*
Go to bed right now!

w: **Ikun yattara, mō ikii ya.**
e: *Ikun nara, mō ikinasai.*
If you're going to go, then go now.

w: **Hayō shinasai!/Hayō shii yo!**
e: *Hayaku shinasai!*

Hurry up!/Do it quickly!

w: **Ē kagen ni se ya! /Ē kagen ni se! /Ē kagen ni shii!**
e: *Ii kagen ni shiro!*
Cut it out!/ For God's sake stop it!

The above might be said to stop two people who are fist fighting.

w: **Ashita no pātii ikantokō.**
e: *Ashita no pātii iku no yosō.*
Let's forget about going to tomorrow's party.

w: **Anata wa itsumo yoru hayō kaette kōhen kara rikon shitai.**
e: *Anata wa itsumo yoru hayaku kaette konai kara rikon shitai.*
You never come home early, so I want a divorce.

w: **Asu hatarakun chau?**
e: *Ashita hatarakun ja nai?*
You're working tomorrow, right?

w: **Boku no jitensha wa pakurareta.**
e: *Boku no jitensha wa nusumareta.*
My bike was stolen.

Pakuru is the Western Japanese word for "to steal."

w: **A: Anta eki made nande ittan?**
B: Aruite itteten.
e: *A: Anata eki made dō yatte itta no?*
B: Aruite itta.
A: How did you get to the station?
B: I walked.

w: **Ashita ame yattara dō shō mo nai de.**
e: *Ashita ame dattara dō shiyō mo nai ne.*
If it rains tomorrow we're out of luck.

w: **Anta nani amaeten no.**
e: *Anata nani amaeteru no.*
Don't act spoiled.

Kansai Love

It is not unusual for a cool city girl anywhere in Japan to play the field before marriage and thus have several boyfriends. The one she uses for his slick car is her *asshikun.* This derives from the slang use of *ashi* to mean "car." The one she uses for sex is her *nesshikun* which derives from *neru,* "to sleep." The one she uses to buy her food and things is her *messhikun,* because *meshi* is slang for "food." And the boyfriend she keeps around in case all the other guys catch on to the fact that they are being used she calls her *kiipukun,* which derives from the English word "keep." Japanese girls are not always as naive as they pretend to be.

w: **Ashi ga an nen yanka.**
e: *Ashi ga arun da yo.*
He has a car you know.

Aru often gets abbreviated to *an* in Western Japanese.

w: **Koibito ga on nen yanka.**
e: *Koibito ga irun da yo.*
He has a girlfriend./She has a boyfriend.

Koibito, literally "love person," can be used to refer to either sex. *Oru,* the Western Japanese word for *iru,* can be abbreviated to *on.* Reducing *-ru* to *-n* is one of the most common abbreviations in Japanese slang, regardless of region.

w: **Dare mo orehen kara ē yan.**
e: *Dare mo inai kara daijōbu da yo.*
Nobody's here, so it's O.K.

Variations of *oru* include: *orehen* (Ōsaka), *orahen* (Kyōto), *ottehen* (Kōbe), and *oran* (Chūgoku). Other verbs follow this pattern.

w: **Ano ko ga henji shite mo sendemo, boku no ai (wa) kawarehen nen.**
e: *Ano ko ga henji shite mo shinakute mo, boku no ai kawaranain da yo.*
No matter whether she replies or not, my love for her will never change.

There are two common verbs meaning "to do": *yaru* and *suru. Suru* is usually used for other people's actions, and *yaru* for one's own actions. *Yaru* can also be used for the actions of people with whom one is on very intimate terms, but keep in mind that it has an informal and sometimes rough nuance.

w: **Watashi ga benkyō yatte mo yarande mo tesuto wa ē ten toreru.**
e: *Watashi ga benkyō yatte mo yaranakute mo tesuto wa ii ten ga toreru.*
Whether I study or not I'll get a good score on the test.

w: **Ano ko kara henji morōte mo morawande mo kamahen.**
e: *Ano ko kara henji moratte mo morawanakute mo kamawanai.*
I don't care whether she replies or not.

w: **Atashi ochikonden nen.**
e: *Atashi ochikonderu no yo.*
I'm depressed.

w: **Anta no koto daisuki ya wa.** ♀
e: *Anata no koto daisuki.*
I'm crazy about you.

w: **Suki (kirai) ya nen./Sukkyanen.**
e: *Suki (kirai) desu.*
I like (hate) it.

w: **Iya ya.**
e: *Iya da.*
Stop it./It bothers me.

w: **Busu dokoro ka beppin ya.**
e: *Busu dokoro ka bijin da.*
Far from being ugly, she's beautiful.

w: **Masaka Naoko ga rezu ya nante.**
e: *Masaka Naoko ga rezu da nante.*
I really doubt that Naoko's a lesbian.

Masaka means an indignant "I don't believe it!" *Rezu* derives from "lesbian." Words for gay men in Japanese include *gei-boi, homo, onna-girai,* and *okama.*

w: **Kanojo mō san-jussai ya nante.**
e: *Kanojo mō san-jussai da nante.*
I can't believe she's already thirty.

w: **yomesan/yomehan/uchi no yomesan**
e: *nyōbō/kanai (formal)*
my wife

A respectful word for one's own wife is *tsuma.* It is symptomatic of Japan's pervading sexism *(danson-johi)* that men commonly refer to their wives as *kanai* (literally "in-the-house"), whereas women mostly refer to their husbands as *shujin* or *danna* (both meaning "master"). When referring to another person's wife, use *okusan,* and when referring to another person's husband, use *goshujin* or *dannasan.*

w: **Musuko ga tonari no musume to kakeochi shiyotta.**
e: *Musuko ga tonari no musume to kakeochi shita.*
The son eloped with the girl next door.

w: **A: Nande sonna ureshisō na kao shiten no?**
B: Anta kirei ya yuwarete yorokonden nen.
e: *A: Dōshite sonna (ni) ureshisō na kao shiten no?*
B: Anata kirei da to iwarete yorokonden no yo.
A: Why do you look so happy?
B: I was told I look pretty, so I feel happy.

w: **Omae nan ya nen?** ♂
e: *Omae nan dai?*
What are you?

w: **Muchakucha majime na ko ya.**
e: *Sugoku majime na ko da.*
He's super serious.

w: **Ē aite mitsukena (akan).**
e: *Ii aite mitsukenai to (ikenai).*
You've got to find a good partner.

w: **Jinsei (o) tanoshimana son ya.**
e: *Jinsei (o) tanoshimanai to son da.*
If you don't enjoy life it's a waste.

w: **Ā yū o-seji (wa) iran.**
e: *Ā yū o-seji wa iranai.*
I don't need that kind of flattery.

w: **Kakko ē na! Kitto moteru yaro.**
e: *Kakko ii ne! Kitto moteru daro.*
He's gorgeous! I bet he's really popular.

w: **Gyūtto daite.**
e: *Gutto daite./ Dakishimete.*
Hug me close.

w/e: ***Yakimochi yaiten no?***
Are you jealous?

w: **Mō naretan ya.**
e: *Mō nareta yo.*
I'm already used to it.

w: **Anta yakimochi yō yaku ne.**
e: *Anata (wa) yakimochi yoku yaku ne.*
You get jealous easily, don't you?

w: **Nani urayamashigatten no!**

e: *Nani urayamashigatten no yo!* ♀/*Nani urayamashigatten dai?* ♂

What are you acting jealous for!

w: **Kawaisō ya.**

e: *Kawaisō da.*

It's pathetic./It's pitiful.

w: **Ikiteru uchi ni aisana sabishii.**

e: *Ikiteru uchi ni aisanai to sabishii.*

It would be sad not to love while one is still living.

w: **Shinjirarehen.**

e: *Shinjirarenai.*

It's incredible./I don't believe it.

w: **Ano futari mō ni-nen-kan tsukiatteru kedo, saikin anmari naka yō nai wa.**

e: *Ano futari mō ni-nen-kan tsukiatteru kedo, saikin anmari naka yoku nai ne.*

Those two have been going out for two years already, but lately they haven't been getting along too well.

w: **Anta kekkon shihatta 'te kiita wa.**

e: *Anata kekkon shita 'tte kiita yo.*

I heard that you got married.

w: **Kanojo no koto anmari suki to chau wa.**

e: *Kanojo no koto anmari suki ja nai.*

I really don't like her very much.

w/e: ***Hajimete anata to kisu shita toki, dokitto shita.***

The first time I kissed you my heart was pounding.

w/e: ***Donogurai no ōkisa?/Donna ōkisa?***
How big?

w: **Dekai./Monosugoi ōkii.**
e: *Monosugoku ōkii.*
It's huge.

w: **Chitchai.**
e: *Chitchai desu.*
It's tiny.

w: **Kimochi ē wa.**
e: *Kimochi ii.*
It feels great.

w: **Kosobai ya.**
e: *Kusuguttai.*
That tickles.

w: **Omae ga soba ni oru to shiawase ya.** ♂
e: *Kimi ga soba ni iru to shiawase da yo.*
When you're next to me I feel happy.

w: **Yarashisō na kao sentoite ya!**
e: *Iyarashisō na kao (o) shinaide!*
Stop looking at me that way!

w: **Ore wa honki de kanojo ni horetenai kedo onna ga soba ni oru hō ga ē nen.**
e: *Boku wa honki de kanojo (o) aishitenai. Dakedo onna ga soba ni iru hō ga ii kara ne.*
I'm not seriously in love with her, but it's better to have a girl at my side than not.

w: **Hitomebore yatta.**
e: *Hitomebore datta.*
It was love at first sight.

w: **Aishitoru.** ♂/**Aishiteru.** ♀
e: *Aishiteru.*
I love you.

This is deep love, not to be said lightly anywhere in Japan. If you mean "I'm really into you" or "I'm crazy about you," you can say *anata no koto ga (dai)suki* or *anata ni muchū da*. Because *aishiteru* sounds so intense, people in Western Japan tend to say the following instead:

w: **Omae ni horetoru.** ♂/**Anta ni horeteru.** ♀
e: *Anata ni horete iru.*
I love you.

w: **Anta no koto sukkyanen.**
e: *Kimi no koto suki da yo.* ♂/*Anata no koto suki desu.* ♀
I'm nuts about you.

w: **Anta (wa) taisetsu na hito ya.**
e: *Anata wa taisetsu na hito da.*
You're really important to me.

w: **Kyō wa seiribi yakara, sekkusu dekihin nen.**
e: *Kyō wa seiribi dakara, sekkusu dekinai no.*
Today I have my period so I can't have sex.

w: **Ore no kodomo oroshitara akan.**
e: *Ore no kodomo oroshitcha dame.*
Don't abort my baby.

Because the pill *(piru)* and other forms of female contraception *(hinin)* are hard to get in Japan, Japanese women have abortions at a shockingly high rate. Some say that the medical industry lobbies hard to keep the pill off the general market because abortion is so lucrative for doctors. True or not, the only readily available protection is still the *kondomu.*

w/e: ***Chiyahoya sareru no ga suki.***
I like being worshiped by members of the opposite sex.

w: **Nugashite.**
e: *Nugasete.*
Take off my clothes.

w: **Anta to shitai.**
e: *Anata to netai.*
I want to sleep with you.

w: **Dekitan ka na?**
e: *Dekita no ka na?*
I wonder if I'm pregnant.

w: **A: Atashi no orahen uchi ni, mata uwaki shita mitai.**
B: Uragirareterun to chau?
e: *A: Atashi no inai toki ni, mata uwaki shita mitai.*
B: Uragirareterun ja nai?
A: It looks like he cheated on me again while I was away.
B: You're being betrayed, aren't you?

w: **Watashi wa hokasaretan ya.**
e: *Watashi wa suterareta.*
I was dumped.

w: **Watashi wa hottokaretan ya.**

e: *Watashi wa oite ikareta.*
He (she) left me.

w: **A: Anta konogoro ē kareshi dekita yaro.**
B: Un, sō. Mō kon'yaku shiten nen.
e: *A: Anata wa saikin ii kareshi dekita deshō.*
B: E, sō desu. Mō kon'yaku shitemasu.
A: Seems you got a new boyfriend recently.
B: That's right. We're already engaged.

Be careful not to confuse *kon'yaku* (engagement) *konnyaku* (a kind of tasteless jelly often found in Japanese dishes) and *konyakku* (cognac). Have a native speaker say the three words to you consecutively. You know you're making progress when they stop sounding identical.

w: **Wakaretanai kedo, jiyū ni sashitaru yo.** ♂
e: *Wakaretakunai kedo, jiyū ni sasete ageru yo.* ♂
I don't want to break up, but I'll let you be free.

Two Teenage Girls in Kobe

Western Japanese

A: Kyō nichiyō ya nā.
B: Sō ieba sō ya nā.
A: Nā, anmari tenki ē koto nai kara kaimon demo iko ka?
B: Mm, iko iko. Atashi sukāto hoshii nen.
A: Sō ieba Ōpa de bāgen yatteru kara soko iko ka?
B: Saki ni gohan tabete kara na.

Kissaten de:
A: Anta nani suru?
B: Watashi mōningu ni suru wa.
A: Honnara watashi mo sō suru wa.

Waiter: Irasshaimasse.
A: Mōningu futatsu.
Waiter: Hai, shōshō omachi kudasai.
B: Yan, chotto mita? Ima no ko mechamecha kakko ē yan.
A: So ka nā. Betsu ni sonna ni kakko ē to omoehen kedo.
B: Uso ya! Ano ko atashi no taipu ya wa.
A: Shōkai shitaro ka?
B: Uso! Anta ano ko no koto shitten no?
A: Mm. Oniichan ya nen.
B: Honmakaina!

EASTERN JAPANESE

A: Kyō wa nichiyōbi yo ne.
B: Sō ieba sō ne.
A: O-tenki wa amari yokunai kara shoppingu demo ikō ka?
B: Mm, ikō. Watashi wa sukāto ga hoshii no.
A: So ieba Ōpa de bāgen shiteiru kara soko ni ikō yo.
B: Mazu gohan o tabete kara ne.

Kissaten de:
A: Anata wa nani ni suru no?
B: Watashi wa mōningu ni suru wa.
A: Ja watashi mo sō suru wa.
Waiter: Irasshaimase.
A: Mōningu o futatsu.
Waiter: Hai, shōshō omachi kudasai.
B: Chotto mita? Ima no ko sugoku kakko ii wa ne.
A: Sō kashira. Betsu ni sonna ni kakko ii to omowanai kedo.
B: Sō kashira! Ano ko wa watashi no taipu da wa.
A: Shōkai shite ageyō ka?
B: Uso! Anata ano ko o shitten no?
A: Datte, oniichan da mon.
B: Uso bakkari!

English

A: Today's Sunday, isn't it?

B: Yeah, I guess so.

A: You know, the weather's not so nice. How about going shopping or something?

B: Yeah, let's go. I want to get a skirt.

A: Well, since there's a sale at Ōpa (a shopping plaza in Kōbe), let's go there.

B: Let's go eat first.

At a cafe:

A: What are you going to have?

B: I'm going to get the morning set.

A: If you get that I guess I will too.

Waiter: Hi. What can I get for you?

A: We'll have two morning sets.

Waiter: I'll be right back.

B: Wow, did you notice? That guy's really cute.

A: You think so? I don't think he's all that good-looking.

B: You've got to be kidding. That guy's my type for sure.

A: Want me to introduce him to you?

B: Get out of here! Do you know him?

A: Yeah, he's my older brother.

B: Yeah, right!

Two High School Boys in Ōsaka

Kōshien refers to the baseball stadium where the high school baseball championships are played. It seems that half the country can't tear itself away from the tube during this annual summer event.

Western Japanese

A: Os!

B: Os!
A: Kinō no Kōshien dotchi ga katten?
B: Tenri ya.
A: Nan tai nan yatten?
B: Ichi-zero ya.
A: Oshikatta nā.
B: Dotchi o ōen shiteten?
A: Sora Okinawa ya, yappari.
B: Sora dō demo ē kedo, Chieko to wa donai natten nen?
A: Ore ni horetoru mitai ya nen kedo, nanka yō wakarahen nen. Anmari jibun o misehen nen.
B: Hakkiri kiite mi.
A: Chō hazukashii kedo nā, yatte miru wa.
B: Ganbare ya.
A: O, ganbaru wa.
B: Honara na!
A: Uh.

Eastern Japanese:
A: Os!
B: Os!
A: Kinō no Kōshien dotchi ga katta?
B: Tenri da.
A: Nan tai nan datta?
B: Ichi-zero da.
A: Oshikatta nā.
B: Dotchi o ōen shiteta?
A: Sore wa Okinawa da yo, yappa.
B: Tokoro de sa, Chieko to wa dō natten dai?
A: Ore ni horeteru mitai nan da kedo sa, yoku wakaranain da. Amari jibun o misenai kara.
B: Hakkiri kiite miro yo.
A: Chotto hazukashii kedo nā, yatte miru.
B: Ganbare.

A: Ganbaru zo.
B: Ja na.
A: Uh.

English

A: Hey.
B: Hey man.
A: Who won at Kōshien yesterday?
B: Tenri did.
A: What was the final score?
B: One to nothing.
A: Wow, that was close.
B: Who did you want to win?
A: Okinawa of course.
B: Well, anyway, how are things turning out with Chieko?
A: It looks like she's crazy about me, but I'm not too sure. She doesn't show too much of herself.

B: Just ask her.
A: I guess I'm sort of shy, but I'll try.
B: Go for it.
A: O.K. I will
B: O.K. See ya.
A: Yeah.

3

KYŌTO STYLE

Kyōto Japanese is renowned for its elegance. Influenced by Kyōto's thousand years as the political capital, the traditional language of Kyōto is rich in polite expressions. Many such expressions have become obscure and are now used almost exclusively by Kyōto's small upper class, geisha, and other guardians of ancient court culture. For example, when a high-class woman such as a *geisha* or *maiko* (geisha in training) speaks, she calls herself *uchi* and replaces *desu* with *dosu*.

In the example sentences in this chapter, (w) stands for Kyōto-style Western Japanese.

w: **Uchi no namae wa Chieko dosu.**
e: *Watashi no namae wa Chieko desu.*
My name is Chieko.

w: **Kirei dosu e.**
e: *Kirei desu yo.*
It's pretty.

Notice the way *-san* becomes a softer *-han* in the courtly Kyōto style.

w: **Naoko-han kirei doshita.**
e: *Naoko-san kirei deshita.*
Naoko was pretty.

Although young Kyōto people speak more or less standard Western Japanese, the traditional language is far from dead. Older people continue to speak elegantly. To young ears this style of talking sounds almost effeminate, such as when *-nasai* is replaced with *-yasu.*

w: **Gomenyasu./Sunmahen.**
e: *Gomen nasai./O-jama shimasu.*
Sorry./Excuse me. (Also used to mean "Hello, is anybody in?")

w: **Okoshiyasu!/ Oideyasu!**
e: *Irasshai!*
Welcome! Come in! (at stores and restaurants)

w: **Omedetō san dosu!**

e: *Omedetō gozaimasu!*
Congratulations!

In Kyōto speech, *kudasai* is replaced with *okureyasu,* particularly in the speech of older ladies.

w: **Mō netōkureyasu.**
e: *Mō nete kudasai.*
Please go to bed.

w: **Chotto hayō tabetōkureyasu.**
e: *Chotto hayaku tabete kudasai.*
Please eat a little faster.

Geisha may use the following very polite expression.

w: **Chotto o-machi yashito okureyasu.**
e: *Chotto o-machi kudasai.*
Please wait a moment.

In several expressions *dosu* is abbreviated to *osu.*

w: **Atsu osu na.**
e: *Atsui desu ne.*
Hot, isn't it.

w: **Kinō samu oshita na.**
e: *Kinō samukatta ne.*
It was cold yesterday, wasn't it.

w: **Oido ga ito osu nen.** (*Oido* is a polite word for "rump.")
e: *Oshiri ga itain desu.*
My bottom hurts.

w: **Omoshiro oshita./Okashi oshita.**

e: *Omoshirokatta./Okashikatta.*
It was funny.

Omoshiroi is used to mean funny or interesting in the sense of entertaining. *Okashii* is used to mean funny in the sense of weird or laughable.

In Western Japan, there are often two different forms of a given verb, both having the same meaning, such as *kakahen* and *kakehen* (don't write), or *ikahen* and *ikehen* (don't go). In general, the *a* form is more prevalent in Kyōto, and the *e* form is more prevalent in Ōsaka.

w: **A: Ashita iku?**
B: Ikahen nen.
e: *A: Ashita iku?*
B: Ikanai.
A: Are you going tomorrow?
B: No, I'm not.

w: **A: Raishū iku?**
B: Ikehen nen./Ikarehen nen.
e: *A: Raishū iku?*
B: Ikenai.
A: Are you going next week?
B: I can't.

Throughout Western Japan the negative tense of the verb is formed by adding either *-hen* or *-n.* The *-n* form is more common the further west you go, with the *-hen* form most prevalent in Kyōto and Ōsaka. However, both forms are in common usage throughout Western Japan. Some examples are *oran* and *orahen/orehen* (is not), *ikan* and *ikahen/ikehen* (don't go), and *taben* and *tabehen* (don't eat).

w: **Kyōbi no wakai mon no kangae wakaran wa.**
e: *Chikagoro no wakamono no kangae wa wakaranai.*
I just don't understand the way young people think nowadays.

w: **Ore wa ikan te yūtan ya de./Ore wa ikan te yūta yan.**
e: *Ore wa ikanai 'te itta yo.*
I told you I wouldn't go.

POLITE KYŌTO LANGUAGE

Other features having an origin in the language of Kyōto's ancient court culture have found their way into everyday language and can be heard throughout Western Japan. One common example is the *-haru* verb ending, which is used all over Western Japan but is especially heard in Kyōto. This ending has no meaning as such and no exact equivalent in Eastern Japanese, but it makes verbs pleasantly polite. For example:

w: **Anta gorufu shiharu?**
e: *Anata gorufu saremasu ka?*
Will you go golfing?

w: **Otōsan iharimasu ka?**
e: *Otōsan irassharu?/Otōsan oraremasu ka?*
Is your father in?

You would say the above phrase and not the formal *otōsan irasshaimasu ka?* to a kid on the phone.

w: **Doko ni sundeharun desu ka?**
e: *Doko ni sunde imasu ka?*
Where do you live?

Note that *sundeharu* is not nearly as polite as *sunde irasshaimasu* or *sumaremasu*. However, *sundeharu* is more polite than *sunde imasu*. *Sundeharu* conveys respect without the distance or sense of ritual formality that *sunde irasshaimasu* has.

Two Office Women In Kyōto

In the following conversation two women are speaking informally at the office, and then at a pub.

Polite Kyōto Style

A: Otsukaresama desu.
B: Otsukare.
A: Kyō wa zangyō nain desu ka?
B: Un, saikin hima ya kara ne.
A: Massugu kaeraharun desu ka?
B: Sono tsumori ya kedo.
A: Soshitara kyō nomi ni ikimashō ka?
B: Iko, iko.

Robata de:
A: Gōruden uiiku wa dokka ikaharun desu ka?
B: Hawai ni demo ikō ka to omotten nen kedo.
A: Yoyaku wa mō shihattan desu ka?
B: Mada. Ii ryokōgaisha ga mitsukattehen nen.

A: Tsuā de ikaharun desu ka?
B: Ūn, hitori de ikō to omotten nen.
A: Ā nanika kitai shiteharimasu ne.
B: Ā, wakatta?
A: Ima, ichiban yasui chiketto de ikura gurai kakarun desu ka?
B: Mā, jū-man-en gurai ya ne.

EASTERN JAPANESE
A: Otsukaresama.
B: Otsukare.
A: Kyō wa zangyō nain desu ka?
B: Un, saikin hima da kara ne.
A: Massugu kaerun desu ka?
B: Sono tsumori da kedo.
A: Sore ja, kyō nomi ni ikimashō ka?
B: Un, ikō.

Robata de:
A: Gōruden uiiku wa doko ka ikun desu ka?
B: Hawai ni demo ikō ka to omotterun da kedo.
A: Yoyaku wa mō shiterun desu ka?
B: Mada. Ii ryokōgaisha ga mitsukaranain da wa.
A: Tsuā de ikun desu ka?
B: Un. Hitori de ikō to omotte iru no yo.
A: A nani ka kitai shiterun desu ne.
B: A, wakatta?
A: Ima ichiban yasui chiketto de ikura gurai kakarun desu ka?
B: Mā, jū-man-en gurai ne.

ENGLISH
A: You've had a long day.
B: You too.
A: Are you doing any overtime today?
B: No, lately I've had a lot of free time.

A: Will you head straight home?
B: Well I was planning to, but . . .
A: Well then, would you like to go and have a drink?
B: Sure, let's go.

At a pub:
A: Are you going to go somewhere during Golden Week?
B: I'm thinking of going to Hawaii or somewhere.
A: Have you already made reservations?
B: Not yet. I haven't found a good travel agent.
A: Are you going to go as part of a tour?
B: No, I'm planning to go alone.
A: I bet you're hoping to get lucky.
B: How'd you guess?
A: What's the cheapest ticket going for now?
B: Oh, around 100,000 yen.

HARU REVIEW

The following table should make clear how *-haru* verbs are constructed:

Kyōto Style	Standard Japanese
ikaharimasu	*ikimasu*
ikaharimashita	*ikimashita*
ikahattan desu	*ittan desu*
ikahattan yarō	*ittan darō*
ikahatta	*itta*
ikaharu	*iku*
ikahan no?	*iku no?*
ittahatta	*itte ita*

w: **A: Eiga o miharu no?**
B: Mitai kedo, tegami kakan to.
e: *A: Eiga o miru no?*
B: Mitai kedo, tegami (o) kakanai to.
A: Will you watch the movie?
B: I want to, but I have to write a letter.

w: Shachō-san dekaketehatta no?
e: Shachō-san dekakete oraremashita no?
Did you go out (and come back)? (Said to a company president)

w: A: Shachō-san mō dekakehatta no?
B: Chigaimasu. Chotto seki hazushite harimasu.
e: A: Shachō-san mō dekakerareta no?
B: Chigaimasu. Chotto seki hazushite imasu.
A: Did the president leave already?
B: No. He (she) is momentarily away from his (her) desk.

The *gozaimasu* form is frequently used in Kyōto Japanese. Actually, this form may have been borrowed into Eastern Japanese from Western Japanese way back when Kyōto was still the capital. This would account for the transformation that adjectives undergo before *gozaimasu* and the fact that Eastern Japanese uses the same form as Western Japanese.

w/e: ***Yō gozaimasu.***
It is good.

w/e: ***Takō gozaimasu.***
It is high.

w/e: ***O-atsū gozaimasu.***
It is hot.

w/e: ***Yoroshū gozaimasu.***
It is fine.

4

HIROSHIMA STYLE

Hiroshima Japanese is quite similar to Kansai Japanese. The main difference is that the copula *ya* is replaced by *ja*. This is typical of Japanese dialects in far western Honshū.

w: **Kirei jatta, honma ni.**
e: *Kirei datta, honto ni.*
It was really pretty.

w: **Mō ittan ja nō.** ♂ **(Kansai: Mō ittan ya nen.)**
e: *Mō ittan da ne.*
They already left.

w: **Ashita ame ga furun jarō.**
e: *Ashita ame ga furun darō na.*
It'll probably rain tomorrow.

Another important difference between Hiroshima Japanese and Kansai Japanese is that the negative verbs tend to end in *-n* as opposed to *-hen*.

w: **Nanmo tabenkatta. (Kansai: Nanmo tabehenkatta.)**
e: *Nanimo tabenakatta.*
I didn't eat anything.

w: **Sō omowan ka? (Kansai: Sō omowahen ka?)**

e: *Sō omowanai?*
Don't you think so?

w: **Kare tegami kakan jarō. (Kansai: Kare tegami kakehen yarō.)**
e: *Kare (wa) tegami o kakanai darō.*
He probably won't write a letter.

Another difference between Hiroshima Japanese and Kansai Japanese is the "must" form. The word *akan* (lousy) becomes *iken* in Hiroshima.

w: **Hayō ikenya iken. (Kansai: Hayō ikana akan.)**
e: *Hayaku ikanakereba (naranai)./ Hayaku ikanakya (ikenai).*
I've got to go right away.

w: **Tabenya iken. (Kansai: Tabena akan.)**
e: *Tabenakereba naranai./ Tabenakucha./Tabenakya.*
You must eat.

In Western Japan men tend to use *nō* instead of *na* or *ne* for emphasis at the end of their sentences. This is especially so in and around Hiroshima.

w: Atsui nō. ♂
e: *Atsui desu ne.*
Hot, isn't it?

w: Taigi ja nō.
e: *Tsukareta nā.*
I'm tired.

The initial "s" of words often becomes "h" in Western Japanese. This is especially common in Hiroshima Japanese.

w: Hoshitara ne.
e: Soshitara ne.
In that case./Bye.

w: Hō ja nē./Sō ja nē.
e: Sō da ne.
You're right.

w: A hō ka?
e: A sō ka?
Oh, is that so?

Be careful when saying this not to say *Aho ka?* (Are you stupid?)

w: Hon ja nē./Hon jā ne.
e: Jā ne.
O.K. Bye.

w: Genki ni shitoru?/Genki ni shichoru?/Genki ni shiyoru?
e: Genki ni shiteru?
Are you doing well?

The *no* of *Dō shiteru no?* becomes *ne* in women's Hiroshima Japanese. Men use *na* instead.

w: Dō shōrun ne? ♀/**Dō shōrun na?** ♂
e: Dō shiteru no?
How have you been?

"Because" in Hiroshima is *jaken.*

w: Sō jaken. (Kansai: Sō ya sakai ni.)
e: Sō da kara.
That's why.

w: Watashi wa onna jaken, ryōri senya iken.
Watashi wa onna ya sakai, ryōri sena akan. (Kansai)
e: Watashi wa onna da kara, ryōri shinakya.
I have to cook because I'm a woman.

Two Old Aunties in Hiroshima

The following is a typical conversation between two old ladies in Hiroshima.

Hiroshima Japanese

A: Konnichiwa.
B: Konnichiwa.
A: Atsui nē.
B: Honma ja nē.
A: Saikin dō shōrun ne?
B: Bochi bochi ja nē.
A: Kodomo genki ni shitoru?
B: Mm, genki ni shitoru yo. Kodomo wa genki nan ne?
A: Mm, genki yo. Kono bonsai kirei ja nē.
B: Mm. Senshū musuko kōte kureta.
A: Konshūmatsu matsuri ni ikun ne?
B: Uchi wa isogashūte yasumaren.
A: Zannen ja ne.
B: Sore jā ne, hayō kaeranya iken.
A: Sore jā ne.

Eastern Japanese

A: Konnichiwa.
B: A, domo.
A: Atsui desu nē.
B: Honto ni atsui desu nē.
A: Saikin dō shiteru no?
B: Mā mā desu ne.

A: Kodomo wa genki ni shiteru?
B: E, genki ni shiteru wa yo. Kodomo wa genki na no?
A: Genki yo. Kono bonsai kirei desu nē.
B: Mm. Senshū musuko ga katte kureta.
A: Konshūmatsu matsuri ni iku no?
B: Uchi wa isogashikute yasumarenakute.
A: Zannen desu nē.
B: Jā ne, hayaku kaeranakya ikenai kara.
A: Jā ne.

English
A: Good afternoon.
B: Ah, hello.
A: Hot, isn't it?
B: You can say that again.
A: How've you been lately?
B: Not too bad.
A: Are the kids doing well?
B: Sure, they're doing just fine. Are your kids well?
A: They're fine. My, this bonsai is pretty.
B: Yes, my son bought it for me last week.
A: Are you going to go to the festival this weekend?
B: No, I'm busy at home and can't take off.
A: That's too bad.
B: Well, take care. I have to go home now.
A: Yes, goodbye.

5

ŌSAKA STYLE

In Ōsaka there is a traditional way of talking called *Naniwa kotoba. Naniwa* was Ōsaka's name long ago. This style of talking is fairly common among middle-aged and older people, but most young people seem to favor a more standard Kansai Japanese. *Naniwa kotoba* has much in common with the traditional Kyōto way of talking, such as *-yasu* and *-haru* endings, but is less refined. Although you probably wouldn't want to use *Naniwa kotoba* yourself, learning the basics will help you understand gangster and samurai movies, Ōsaka radio and TV, conversations with older people, or the infamous *manzai,* Ōsaka's mile-a-minute comic dialogues. You can hear a radio talk show in strong Ōsaka Japanese in the mornings throughout central Kansai on Mainichi Hōsō, 1179 on the AM dial. A line or two of *Naniwa kotoba* thrown into a conversation at the right time is guaranteed to get some laughs.

In Ōsaka, *-su* is often omitted from verbs. Thus, *desu na* becomes *denna,* and *desu ka* becomes *dekka.*

w: **Atsui denna.**
e: *Atsui desu ne.*
Hot, isn't it.

w: **Ē o-tenki denna.**
e: *Ii o-tenki desu ne.*
Beautiful weather, isn't it.

w: **Bochi bochi denna.**
e: *Mā mā desu ne.*
You know, so so.

Don't confuse *denna* with the *de ne* abbreviation, which means "because."

w: **Minō no kōyō ga kirei de ne, shashin ippai totte kita.**
e: *Minō no kōyō ga kirei na no de, shashin o ippai totte kita.*
The fall foliage in Minō's so pretty, I took plenty of photos.

To make matters more complicated, *desu,* which is itself an abbreviation of *de arimasu,* is often replaced with another verb *de omasu.* (In Kyōto *de arimasu* is replaced with *de osu* which is usually abbreviated into *dosu* or *osu.*) But since *de* and *su* usually get omitted, the expression *omanna* derived from *de omasu na* is often heard.

w: **Samu omanna.**
e: *Samui desu ne.*
Cold, isn't it.

w: **Kore wa honma ni ē koto de omasu na.**
e: *Kore wa honto ni ii koto desu ne.*
This is really a good thing (to have occurred).

w: **Sō de oman.**
e: *Sō desu.*
That's right./Indeed.

w: **Mōshiwake omahen./Mōshiwake arimahen.**
e: *Mōshiwake arimasen.*
I'm sorry./There's no excuse for what I have done.

w: **Gotsuosan de omashita.**
e: *Gochisōsama deshita.*
That was an excellent meal, thank you.

Because *-su* is omitted, verbs often end in *-makka* (from *-masu ka*), *-manna (-masu na), -manya (-masu nya), -mannen (-masu nen), -ma (-masu), or -harimanna (-harimasu na).*

w: **Mōkattemakka?**
e: *Kēki wa dō desu ka?*
How's business?/Are you making a profit?

The usual reply to this question is *Bochi bochi denna* (I'm doing so so).

w: **Wakarimakka?**
e: *Wakarimasu ka?*
Do you understand?

w: **Sensei mō dekaketeharimanna. /Sensei mō dekakete-harimasu ne. (standard Kansai)**
e: *Sensei mō o-dekake ni narimashita yo.*
(The) teacher has already left.

w: **Ittekima.**
e: *Ittekimasu.*
I'm going (and will come back).

Most people say *ittekimasu,* even in Western Japan. However, people with extremely thick Ōsaka accents will usually delete even this *su.*

w: **Mō itteahariman nen ya wa.**
e: *Mō ikimashita./Mō ikaremashita.*
He already left.

w: **Isogashūte bata bata yattemannen.**
e: *Isogashikute bata bata shiterun da.* ♂
I'm so busy, I'm working like crazy.

w: **Watashi kawaii no to chaimannen, kirei dennen.** ♀
e: *Watashi wa kawaii'n ja nakute, kirei na no yo.*
I'm not cute, I'm beautiful.

Chaimannen derives from *chigaimasu nen. Dennen* derives from *desu nen.*

w: **Sunmahen, Seigō-san iteharimakka?**
e: *Sumimasen, Seigō-san irasshaimasu ka?*
Excuse me, is Seigō in?

The verb *arimasu* is frequently replaced with *omasu.* The negatives *arimahen, arehen,* and *omahen* are all commonly heard.

w: **Ē hanashi omahen ka?/ Ē hanashi arimahen ka?**
e: *Ii hanashi arimasen ka?*
Got any good news?

In *Naniwa kotoba* the standard Kansai *ya na* replacement for *desu na* is as common as the *denna* form. In Ōsaka it is fine to express *sō desu ne* as either *sō denna* or *sō ya na.*

w: **Omae wa bentō o motte kite kuretan yate na.** ♂
e: *Kimi wa bentō o motte kite kuretan da 'tte ne.*
I understand that you brought a lunch box for me.

w: **Benkyō shita kate, ukaru no wa muri yarō. /Benkyō shita kate, ukarehen yarō.**
e: *Benkyō shitatte, gōkaku dekinai deshō.*
Even if I study, I probably can't pass.

The traditional Ōsaka equivalent of *desu yo* is *desse.*

w: **Kotoshi no kōyō wa honma ni kirei desse.**
e: *Kotoshi no kōyō wa honto ni kirei da yo.*
This year's fall foliage is really pretty.

As is common throughout Western Japan, adverbs lack *-ku.* For example, *isogashikute* (busily) becomes *isogashiite,* and *hayaku* (quickly) becomes *hayō.*

w: **Hayō shii ya!/Hayō se ya!**
e: *Hayaku shiro!*
Do it fast!/ Hurry up!

w: **Hajimete denna, yoroshū (ni).**
e: *Hajimete desu ne, yoroshiku (ne).*
Nice to meet you.

w: **Osō okite, mada mada neboketen nen.**
e: *Osoku okite, mada mada neboketerun da.*
I got up late and still feel groggy.

w: **Samūte akimahen. (akimahen = akan)**
e: *Samukute dame desu.*
I can't take this cold weather.

Another phrase common to Ōsaka vernacular is *sakai ni,* which is the same as *(da) kara,* meaning "because," or *no de* meaning "so."

w: **Kyō, watashi wa gakkō ni ikarehenkatta sakai ni doko ga shukudai ka wakarehen.**
e: *Kyō, watashi wa gakkō ni ikenakatta no de, doko ga shukudai na no ka wakarimasen.*
I couldn't go to school today, so I don't know what the homework is.

w: **A: Nande sonna aho na koto yūtan ya!?**
B: Ahondara! Omae ga ningen no kuzu ya sakai ya! ♂
e: *A: Dōshite sonna baka na koto ittan dai!?*
B: Baka yaro! Temē ga ningen no kuzu da kara nan da yo! ♂
A: Why did you say such a stupid thing!?
B: You idiot! Because you're human trash, that's why!

w: **A: Omae mō orei shi ni itta ka?** ♂
B: Sonna koto suru hazu nai yaro.
A: Nande ya nen! Sēhen wake ni wa ikahen yaro! Omae (ni wa) giri ga aru nen sakai ni.
e: *A: Omae mō orei shi ni itta?*
B: Suru wake nai jan.
A: Dōshite da yo! Shinai wake ikanai daro! Omae (ni wa) giri ga arun da kara.

A: Did you go and thank (him) yet?
B: C'mon it's not necessary.
A: Why not! You can't not do it! You're indebted (to him).

As mentioned earlier, negative verb forms such as *ikehen* (don't go) and *kakehen* (don't write) are more common in Ōsaka than in Kyōto, where one would say *ikahen* (don't go) and *kakahen* (don't write). However, depending on the speaker, *ikehen* and *kakehen* can also mean "cannot go" and "cannot write," which adds to the confusion. Adding *-arehen,* such as *ikarehen* or *kakarehen,* ensures that the potential case is meant. Many verbs follow this *-arehen* pattern, including *kakarehen* (can't write), *nomarehen* (can't drink), *kawarehen* (can't buy), and *shinarehen* (can't die). It is confusing that verbs like *ikehen* can mean either *ikanai* (don't go) or *ikenai* (can't go) depending on the speaker. Generally, speakers who say *ikehen* to mean "don't go," say *ikarehen* to mean "can't go."

Two Old Men in Ōsaka

The following conversation between two old men in Ōsaka shows how *Naniwa kotoba* sounds in context. Keep in mind that young people would find talking like this very old-fashioned.

Ōsaka Japanese

A: Maido gomenyasu.
B: Ah! Maido!
A: Honma ni hisashiburi dennā!
B: Sō dennā! Isogashūte isogashūte hima arimahen nen. Sō ya kedo nā, kono mae anta ni denwa shiten kedo, daremo deharimahen deshita wa.
A: Honma? Uchi no naka gotsū atsūte, oraremahen nen.
B: Honma ni mushi-atsui dennā.
A: Washira toshiyori ni wa kotaemannā.

B: Honma dennā.

A: Sō ya kedo, mukashi wa senpūki mo arimahen deshita kara nā.

B: Sora sō ya nā.

A: Zeitaku iwaremahen nā.

B: Honde, anta toko mōkattemakka?

A: Bochi bochi dennā. Uchi toko udonya ya kara, kō atsūte wa mōkarimahen wa. Anta toko donai dekka?

B: Anmari ē koto omahen nā. Yappari atarashū dekita sūpā ni makete mau kara nā.

Eastern Japanese

A: Konnichi wa! Jama suru yo!

B: Yā! Yā!

A: Honto ni hisashiburi da nē.

B: Sō da nē. Isogashikute isogashikute hima ga nain da yo. Dakedo sa, kono mae omaesan ni denwa shita kedo, daremo denakatta yo.

A: Honto? Uchi no naka wa sugoku atsukute irarenain da.

B: Honto ni mushi-atsui nē.

A: Washira toshiyori ni wa kotaeru ne.

B: Honto ni sō da ne.

A: Da kedo sa, mukashi wa senpuki mo nakatta kara ne.

B: Sorya sō da na.

A: Zeitaku ienai ne.

B: Tokoro de omaesan no toko hanjō shiteru kai?

A: Mā mā da ne. Uchi wa udonya da kara, konna ni atsukucha mōkaranai yo. Omaesan no toko wa dō ka ne.

B: Amari ii koto nai ne. Yappari atarashiku dekita sūpā ni wa makete shimau kara ne.

ENGLISH

A: Hi. Anybody home?

B: Hi!

A: Been quite a while, hasn't it?

B: Yeah, I've been real busy so I haven't had any free time. I called you recently, but nobody answered the phone.

A: Really? The house is terribly hot, so we can't stay in.

B: It's awful muggy, isn't it.

A: It's tough on us old folks.

B: Yeah, that's for sure.

A: But in the old days we didn't even have electric fans.

B: That's for sure.

A: Can't ask for too much.

B: How's business at your place?

A: So-so. We have an udon shop, so in this heat it's hard to make a buck. How's business with you?

B: Not so great. You know, we just can't compete with the newly built supermarket.

6

TOUGH TALK AND KANSAI CURSES

Throughout Japan, men have a special way of talking when they want to sound masculine, threatening, or strong. Men talk tough with their teammates, friends, girlfriends, and of course during arguments or fights.

Men's tough talk is probably the hardest of all Japanese styles for foreigners to understand let alone master. There are several reasons for this. Apart from the many abbreviations and slang terms used, men tend to slur more and speak more deeply, hoarsely, and quickly when talking tough. They also roll their r's like Spanish when they want to sound especially threatening.

It's probably a good idea not to try to speak tough, except perhaps as a joke, until you feel totally at home in the language. However, you should become familiar with the phrases in this chapter if you want to understand television, movies, and men's talk in general.

Women also speak tough at times, especially women in Western Japan. But women rarely use vulgar language in public, unless harassed. Women usually only use vulgar language when they joke around or get really angry with people they know intimately.

Cursing is not part of everyday Japanese the way it is in slang English. There is nothing comparable to the friendly use of curse words in English, as in "Wow, you scared the shit out of me." In Japanese, cursing is primarily reserved for times when one is really angry or intentionally threatening.

TOUGH TALK

In masculine speech the command form *miseru na!* (don't show me!), is made tougher by abbreviating it into *misenna!* or *misennayo*! This pattern applies to all verbs that end with *-ru.*

w: **Kechi tsukennayo!/Kechi tsukenna ya!** ♂
e: *Monku iu na!/ Monku yūn ja nē yo!*
Don't give me that crap!

w: **A: Kono kinō kōta sēta kirei ya to omowahen?**
B: Nanka yasumon mitai.
A: Itchamon tsukentoite! ♀/ **. . . tsukenna!** ♂
e: *A: Kono kinō katta sēta kirei da to omowanai?*
B: Nanka yasumono mitai.
A: Waruku iwanaide! ♀/ *Waruku iu na!* ♂
A: This sweater I bought yesterday is pretty, don't you think?
B: It looks kind of shoddy.
A: Don't give me your put-downs!

A rougher command than *miseru na* or *misennayo* is *misen ja nai yo.* In tough male talk the *nai* becomes nē. *Misen ja nē yo* means "don't show me!" It is the strongest, crassest command form, and is more common in Eastern than Western Japanese.

w: **Miserun ya nai zo!/Misenna!** ♂
e: *Misen ja nē yo!* ♂
Don't show me!

w/e: ***Namen ja nē yo!*** ♂
Get lost! Fuck off! (literally "don't lick me")

w: **Fuzaken na yo!** ♂
e: *Fuzaken ja nē yo!* ♂
Cut the bullshit!

The standard command form is sometimes different in Western Japanese. For example, *shiro!* (do it!) is often expressed as *shii!* or *shii na!* or *shii ya!* These forms are casually used by both men and women in Western Japan.

w: **Mō nē ya!**
e: *Mō nero!* ♂
Go to bed already!

w: **Hayō shii ya!/Hayō shinasai!/Hayō sē ya!**
e: *Hayaku shiro.* ♂*/Hayaku shinasai!*
Do it quickly!

w: **Mukō mukii aho!**
e: *Atchi muke! Baka!*
Look over there, you fool!

w: **Hayō shine ya!/Shinjimae!**
e: *Hayaku shine!/Shinjimae!* ♂
Drop dead, jerk!

w: **Dete ikii!**
e: *Dete ike!* ♂
Get out!

w: **Yarii ya!/Yare ya!**
e: *Yare!*
Do it!

w: **Atchi ikii!**
e: *Atchi ike!* ♂
Get lost!

Achi ikii! sounds stronger than *achi ikii ya!* in the same way as the

English "get out of here!" sounds stronger than "c'mon, get out of here already!"

w: **Kore yomii!**
e: *Kore yome!* ♂
Read this!

w: **Aho na koto yū na honma ni!** ♂
e: *Baka na koto iu na honto ni!* ♂
Don't talk nonsense!

Instead of *yū na,* a woman in Western Japan might also say *iwantoite* or, if she's more serious, she might say *iwantoki.* In Eastern Japan a woman might say *iwanaide,* which is gentler than *iu na.*

w/e: ***Hottoke!*** ♂/***Hottoite!*** ♀
Lay off!/Stop bugging me!

A command can be made more emphatic in Western Japanese by attaching *-ttore!*

w: **Damare! (Shut up!) → Damattore!** (Shut up and stay shut up!)
w: **Yare! (Do it!) → Yattore!** (Do it and stay at it!)

The informal command form *-te mi!* or *-te mii!* means "go ahead and try it!" It is an abbreviation of *-te miro* but does not sound as rude or abrupt. It is familiar in tone and often used between friends and relatives.

w: **Yatte mi!**
e: *Yatte goran!*
Try it!

w: **Mite mi!**
e: *Mite goran!*
Take a look!

w: **Yūte mi!**
e: *Itte goran!*
Try to say it!

In tough talk the vowel *e* sounds the toughest and most emphatic. Many words are made tougher and more masculine when *e* is substituted for some other vowel, especially in Eastern Japan.

w: **Sugoi!**
e: *Sugē!*
Awesome!

w: **Takai**
e: *Takē!*
Unbelievably expensive!

w: **Itai!**
e: *Itē!*
You're hurting me!/It hurts!

w: **Urusai na!/Urusai yanka!**
e: *Urusēn da yo!* ♂
Stop the noise! Stop pestering me!

w: **Oyaji urusōte nā. Baiku norarehen nen.** ♂
e: *Oyaji urusakute sa. Dakara baiku norenēn da yo.*
My old man is on my back. So I can't ride my motorcycle.

The masculine way to talk about your father is *oyaji* and your mother *ofukuro*. When talking directly to your father you call him *otō-san* or the tough *otō*. Similarly you call your mother *okā-san* or *okā*.

w: **Nan demo nai yo.**
e: *Nan demo nē yo.* ♂
It's nothing.

w: **Sora sō yanke.** ♂
e: *Sorya sō da yo.* ♂
Yeah that's right.

Yanke is the masculine form of *yanka,* a word unique to Kansai, meaning *ja nai ka? Ka,* the question particle, often becomes *ke* in Kansai men's speech.

w: **Mō kutta ke?** ♂
e: *Mō kutta ka?* ♂
Did you already eat?

w: **Shiran.** ♂
e: *Shiranē yo.* ♂
I don't know.

w: **Aitsu konjō nai nā.**
e: *Aitsu konjō nē na.* ♂
He's a coward./He has no guts.

w: **Kō ya nai to akan.**
e: *Kō de nē to dame da.* ♂
It's gotta be like this.

w: **Omae wa saitē no onna ya na!** ♂
e: *Omē (wa) saitē no onna da ze!* ♂
You're a slut!

w/e: ***Uso tsuki!*** ♂
Liar!

The word *kora!* adds a lot of emphasis to a sentence, and is often used when balling someone out. The more the r is rolled the more threatening it sounds. Gangsters, both real and on film often roll their r's like crazy. *Kora!* can also be used alone.

w: **Omae na! Dare ni mukatte mono yutton ja, korra!** ♂
e: *Temē! Dare ni mukatte mono itten da yo, temē!* ♂
Hey you, who the hell do you think you're talking to?

w: **Dotsuitaro ka!** ♂
e: *Naguru zo!* ♂
I'm gonna beat the shit out of you!

Dotsuitaro derives from the Western Japanese verb *dotsuku* (to punch). *Dotsuite yaro ka* is abbreviated into *dotsuitaro ka* and literally means "Shall I give you a punch?" If you're cursing at many people *omae* becomes *omaera*.

w: **Omaera na! Dare ni mukatte mono yutton ja kora! Omaera hara kukutte kenka utten nen yaro na! Washi o dare ya to omoten nen!** ♂
e: *Temēra! Dare ni mukatte mono itten da yo! Temēra hara kukutte kenka utten darō na! Ore o dare da to omotten da!*
Hey assholes, who do you think you're talking to? I'm gonna beat the shit out of you! Who do you think I am!

w: **Omae (wa) nanbo no mon ja!** ♂
e: *Temē nanisama no tsumori da!/Temē nanisama dai!* ♂
I'm not scared of you! (literally "How much of you is there?")

Omae can be either intimate, as between lovers or male buddies, or derogatory, depending on how and when it is used. An even more derogatory word for "you" than *omae* in Western Japanese is *ware.* In Eastern Japanese the equivalent would be *temē* or *kisama,* although the latter isn't much used anymore.

w: **Ware nametottara akan zo, boke!** ♂
e: *Temē baka ni shitara yurusanē zo!* ♂
I won't let you get away with making a fool of me!

w: **Ware nani yatten nen!** ♂
e: *Temē nani shiten dai!* ♂
What the hell are you doing!

w: **Ware nani yūton ja, kora!** ♂
e: *Omae nani itten da!* ♂
What the hell are you saying!

w: **Ware nani miton ja kora!** ♂
e: *Omē nani miten da!* ♂
What the hell are you looking at!

w: **Ahondara!** ♂
e: *Baka yarō!* ♂
Watch it, bonehead!

Note that the *yarō* of *baka yarō,* which means "dimwit," is not the same as the *yarō* of Western Japanese, which means *darō* or "likely." And as with many of these phrases, the degree of threat that comes across depends on the speaker's tone of voice.

w/e: ***Kono yarō!*** ♂
You (that) little rat.

Kono makes it clear that a single person is being pointed out. So whereas *hentai* just means "pervert," *kono hentai* means "you pervert."

w: **Ano yarō washi no onna o totte shimōtan ya.** ♂
e: *Ano yarō ore no onna o tottan da.* ♂
That schmuck stole my girl.

w: **Boke!**
e: *Baka yarō!* ♂
Hey moron!

Boke and *ahondara* mean about the same thing, and are used when you are really serious and ready to fight.

w: **Kusotare!/Kuso!** ♂
e: *Chikushō!/Shimatta!/Kuso!* ♂
Damn it!/Shit!

This is said to yourself after making a mistake. *Kusotare!* can also be used for "Hey shithead!"

w: **Shinde mae!** ♂
e: *Shinjimae!* ♂
Go to hell!

The Western Japanese suffix *-tare* can be attached to a negative word to make a new word that describes a person with such negative characteristics. *Kusotare* thus refers to a person with the attributes of *kuso* (shit).

w: **Ahotare!/Bakatare!** ♂
e: *Bakamon!* ♂
You idiot!

w: **Ahokusa!**
e: *Baka rashii!*
That's absurd!/Don't be ridiculous!

This is said while rolling your eyes in disbelief. It is a friendly put-down.

w: **Aho!**
e: *Baka!*
Fool!/Idiot!

A woman might say *aho* to a leering *chikan* (lecher), *sukebei* (sex fiend), or *hentai* (pervert). If just talking about such a person to somebody else she might use *sukantako* or *sukanhito.*

w: **Sukantako./Sukanhito.**
e: *Iya na hito.*
What a creep.

w: **Nani yatten no, sawarantoite!** ♀
e: *Nani yatten no, sawaranaide!* ♀
What are you doing! Don't touch me!

If a woman were grabbed by a *chikan,* this is what she might say. On the flip side, a woman pervert is called a *chijo.* Just as there are *chikan* on packed trains who grab and touch women, there are *chijo* who touch men.

w: **Yokei na osewa ya!**
e: *Yokei na osewa!*
None of your business!

w: **Dabo!**
e: *Baka!*
Imbecile!

w/e: ***Hottoke!*** ♂/***Hottoite!*** ♀
Bug off!

w/e: ***Bakabakashi./Bakabakashii.***
That's ridiculous.

w: **Anta aho chau?** ♀/**Omae aho chau?** ♂
e: *Anata baka ja nai?* ♀/*Baka ja nē ka?* ♂
You're a fool.

w/e: ***Hetakkuso!***
You're so uncoordinated!

This is said when someone tries to do something physical and fails miserably. For example, if you shoot a basketball and entirely miss the backboard you might be jeered with cries of *hetakkuso!* If you get it in you should be treated to cheers of *umai!*

w: **Nan ya nen kore!**
e: *Nan na no kore!* ♀/*Nan nan dai kore!* ♂
What the hell is this!

w: **Ē kagen ni sei!**
e: *Ii kagen ni shiro!* ♂/*Ii kagen ni shite yo!* ♀
Cut it out!/Stop it!

The above statement would be said, for example, to two people who are fighting.

w: **Ē kagen na koto yū na!** ♂
e: *Ii kagen na koto iu na!* ♂
Don't talk foolishly! Don't talk irresponsibly!

w: **Anta aho mitai.** ♀
e: *Anata wa baka mitai.* ♀
You look like an idiot.

w: **Kono hōkokusho detchiagetan to chau?**
e: *Kono hōkokusho detchiagetan ja nai?*
You bullshitted this report, didn't you?

w: **Share n(i) naran! /Kore 'te share n(i) naran na!**
e: *Jōdan ja nain da zo.* ♂
It's not funny!/What you're doing isn't a joke!

If, for example, children are torturing a turtle or somebody is teasing a retarded person, you could very appropriately say *share naran!* and they would get the message.

There is a particularly tough and vulgar style of speech often used to translate American tough-guy movies into Japanese but almost never actually used in real life, except by gangsters and lowlifes, and by men when they want to seriously offend or threaten. This style is defined by the *yagaru* or *iyagaru* verb ending. It is primarily an Eastern Japanese usage, but can be heard on TV everyday throughout Japan. The more violent the show, the more often *yagaru* is used.

Using this verb ending, *suru* becomes *shiyagaru* and *shite iru* becomes *shiteyagaru. Atsukaimasu* becomes *atsukaiyagaru, atsukatte iru* becomes *atsukatteyagaru,* and so on. Of course you should never use this. If you do, be prepared to fight.

w: **Aitsu mō tabetotta.** ♂
e: *Aitsu mō tabete yagatta./Aitsu mō kutte yagatta.* ♂
He already (fucking) ate.

w: **Ima tabetoru.** ♂
e: *Ima tabete yagaru.* ♂
The asshole's eating right now.

w: **Doko ittotten! Omae nijippun mae ni koko ni iteru hazu yatten zo!** ♂
e: *Doko ni itteyagattan da! Omae wa nijippun mae ni wa koko ni iru hazu dattan da zo!* ♂
Where (the hell) have you been! You were supposed to be here twenty (fucking) minutes ago!

w: **Aitsu honma suke-komashi ya nō. Maiban chau onna to netoru.** ♂
e: *Aitsu wa honto ni suke-komashi da na. Maiban chigau onna to neteyagaru.* ♂
He's a real womanizer. He sleeps with a different girl every (damn) night.

In Western Japan there is a very offensive verb ending *ketsukaru,* which can only be used directly toward the person you are cursing.

w: **Omae hito no onna ni nani shite ketsukannen!** ♂
e: *Temē hito no onna ni nani o shiyagan da yo!* ♂
You shithead, what are you doing messing with my girl!

w: **Omae dare ni mukatte mono yūte ketsukannen!** ♂
e: *Temē dare ni mukatte mono itten da yo!* ♂
Hey butthead, who do you think you're talking to!

w: **Nani shite ketsukannen?** ♂
e: *Nani sun da yo!* ♂
What the hell are you doing?

Two Men Fighting Over a Woman

The following telephone conversation should give an idea of how Japanese men might go about cursing at each other. In this scene, Harada's wife has been sleeping with Yamada. Harada has just found out and calls Yamada to threaten him.

Western Japanese

Harada: Moshi moshi, Yamada ka?
Yamada: Hai sō desu kedo ...
Harada: Washi wa teishu no Harada ya.
Yamada: E! Harada?!
Harada's wife in background: Anta, yamete ya!
Harada to wife: Urusai! Damattore!
Harada's wife in background: Anta ni wa kankei nai yanka!
Harada: Urusai na! Damare! (to Yamada:) Oi! Yamada. Omae nani shite kuretan ya, hito no nyōbō to. Kora! Kiiton no ka? Donai shite kurerun ja!
Yamada: Omae ga jibun no nyōbō hottoku kara akan nen. Okusan anta no koto mō aishitenai 'tte yūtotta.
Harada: Kora. Omae nani yūten nen. Dotsuitaro ka! Korrā!
Yamada: Koreru mon yattara, kite mi!

Harada: Ē ka. Kore ijō koitsu ni chikazuite mi! Kintama hikinuku zo! Wakattan ka, ēh?

Yamada: Fun. (Both slam their receivers down).

EASTERN JAPANESE

Harada: Moshi moshi, Yamada ka?

Yamada: Hai sō desu kedo . . .

Harada: Ore wa teishu no Harada da.

Yamada: E! Harada?!

Harada's wife in background: Anata yamete!

Harada to his wife: Damattero!

Harada's wife in background: Anata ni wa kankei nai koto da wa!

Harada: Urusē! Damattero! (to Yamada:) Oi! Yamada. Omē nani shite kuretan da, hito no nyōbō ni. Kiiten no ka? Dō shite kurerun da!

Yamada: Anta ga jibun no nyōbō hitori ni shitoku kara ikenēn daro. Okusan wa mō anta no koto aishitenai 'tte itteta zo.
Harada: Omē nani itten da. Naguritobasu zo!
Yamada: Koreru mon nara kite miro!
Harada: Ii ka. Kore ijō koitsu ni chikazuite miro! Omae no kintama hikkonuku kara na! Wakatta na!!
Yamada: Fun. (Both slam their receivers down).

ENGLISH
Harada: Hello, Yamada, is that you?
Yamada: Yes, that's right.
Harada: It's me, Harada's husband.
Yamada: Huh!? Harada?
Harada's wife in background: Stop it will you!
Harada: You shut up!
Harada's wife in background: But it has nothing to do with you!
Harada: I said shut up! (to Yamada:) Hey Yamada! What the hell are you doing with another man's wife? Listen! Did you hear me? What are you going to do about this?
Yamada: The way you ignore your wife stinks. Your wife told me she doesn't love you any more.
Harada: What the hell are you saying? I'll beat the shit out of you!
Yamada: If you've got the courage come over. I dare you!
Harada: All right. Just try to come near her again. I'll cut your balls off! You understand!?
Yamada: Hah. (Both slam their receivers down).

7

KANSAI DESCRIPTIONS

Western Japanese is rich with words that describe colorful situations and people. Most of these seem to dwell on negative traits. There is no shortage of words for creeps, brats, morons, and lechers. However, some, such as *gotsui* or *pittashi,* can be very positive.

SUPER!

In Tokyo, when you hear or see something great you say *sugoi!* In Western Japan, women also say *sugoi* but men more often say *gotsui!* or *gotsui ē!*

w: **Gotsui!**
e: *Sugoi!*
Great!

w: **Kono shashin gotsui ē!**
e: *Kono shashin sugoi desu ne!*
This picture's awesome huh!

Gotsui can also mean being physically big.

w: **Gotsui.**
e: *Gatchiri shite iru.*
He's sturdily built.

w: **Nā! Aitsu gotsui na!** ♂
e: *Aitsu gatchiri shiteru ne!* ♂
Wow, he's well-built!

w: **Pittashi.**
e: *Pittari.*
A perfect fit.

w: **Kono sukāto atashi ni pittashi yan.** ♀
e: *Kono sukāto atashi ni pittari da wa.* ♀
This skirt fits me perfectly.

Batchiri is more emphatic than *pittashi* or *pittari*. In Western Japanese there is a tendency to replace *-ri* with *-shi* to add emphasis. So, for example, *yappari,* which means "it figures," becomes *yappashi, pittari* becomes *pittashi,* and *batchiri* becomes *batchishi.*

In general, Japanese words are emphasized by doubling consonants. For example, *yappari* is more emphatic than the alternative form *yahari. Nippon* is more emphatic than *Nihon.* In Eastern Japanese, double consonants are crisp and somewhat more common, but in Western Japanese, double consonants are not overly vocalized unless a specific emphasis of meaning is intended.

Another very non-English way of emphasizing in Japanese is pausing between syllables. For example, *shinjirarehen* (I can't believe it) becomes more emphatic by pausing and contorting your face appropriately: *shin . . . jirarehen.* To create a similar effect, an English speaker would probably increase the volume of a particular word: "I DON'T believe it." In Japanese, words are not usually emphasized by varying loudness but by varying pitch, or by drawing out certain sounds. Varying the loudness of syllables within words is a mistake that most foreigners never get quite right.

Not So Super

If you are asked how your work is going, or how you are doing, and you want to give a vague or unenthusiastic reply, you might say:

w: **Bochi bochi ya ne.**
e: *Mā mā desu ne.*
You know, so so.

w: **Chūto-hanpa ni yattara umaku ikahen yarō.**
e: *Chūto-hanpa ni shitara umaku ikanai darō.*
If you leave things half done, they won't work out well.

w: **Aitsu wa honma ē kagen na ningen ya.**
e: *Aitsu wa honto ni ii kagen na ningen da.*
He's really a lowlife.

Brats

When a *yanchana gaki* (a naughty brat) gets on your nerves so much that you want to scream, you can shut the little monster up by saying:

w: **Yancha yattara akan de!**
e: *Itazura shicha dame da yo!*
No horsing around!/Stop being a brat.

w: **Yancha ya nā.**
e: *Itazura da nā.*
You're a devil.

w: **Aitsu yancha na ko ya./Aitsu yancha na gaki ya.**
e: *Aitsu itazurakko da./Aitsu itazura na gaki da.*
He's a naughty little devil.

In Western Japan, *yancha* has a slightly humorous feeling about it that the next word *gonta* does not.

w: **gonta/gontakure**
e: *warugaki*
a brat

w: **Aitsu honma gonta ya na.** ♂
e: *Aitsu honto ni warugaki desu ne.* ♂
That little brat sure is a monster.

IRRITATING PEOPLE

Japan has its fair share of irritating people. To describe them there are a number of terms that begin with *kuso* (shit).

w/e: ***kusogaki***
a fresh kid/a brat

If the neighbor's kid writes in chalk on your sidewalk and you erase it and he does it again after you told him not to, you might say:

w: **Kono kusogaki mata rakugaki shiyotta na!** ♂
e: *Kono kusogaki mata rakugaki shita na!* ♂
That little brat scribbled again!

w/e: ***kusojiji***
old fart

w/e: ***kusobaba***
old biddy

w/e: ***Kusotare!***
Hey, shithead!

w: **ikezu na hito**
e: *ijiwaru na hito*
a mean-spirited person

w: **Ano ko 'te ikezu na ko ya na.**
e: *Ano ko'tte ijiwaru na ko da ne.*
That girl (guy) is cruel.

If somebody says something nasty and uncalled for you can turn to him and say *ikezu!* with great effect.

TEASERS AND SEX FIENDS

An *ichibiri* in Western Japanese is a person who likes to play stupid practical jokes or tease people in inane ways. For example, one kid pretends to offer some ice cream to a friend and just as she's about to eat it he puts it in his own mouth and laughs hysterically. She might then say *Anta ichibiri ya* and turn and pout, or she might say *Anta nani ichibitten nen,* which is the equivalent verb form. Be careful not to confuse *ichibiri* with *ijimekko.* An *ijimekko* is a bully, and *ijimerarekko* is the kid who always gets beat up by the bully.

w: **ichibiru**
e: *fuzakeru*
to tease tormentingly

The Eastern Japanese verb *karakau* means to tease mockingly or to make fun of someone. In Western Japanese the verb used is *ochokuru.*

w: **Kare kekkon shitai 'te yū nen, atashi o ochokutten no ka na?** ♀
e: *Kare kekkon shitai 'tte iu no, atashi o karakatteru no kashira?* ♀
I wonder if he's just toying with me when he says he wants to marry me.

Both in Western and Eastern Japan, *jirasu* means to tease tantalizingly by keeping a person in suspense. Thus if you want your lover to make love more slowly or teasingly, say *Mō chotto jirashitara kanjiru.* In contrast, a woman who teases a man with no real intention of going to bed with him is called an *omowaseburi na onna.*

w: **A: Ano onna ore ni horeteru mitai ya wa.** ♂
B: Sō ka na. Tada omowaseburi na taido o shiteru dake to chau ka? ♂
e: *A: Ano onna ore ni horeteru mitai nan da.* ♂
B: Sō ka na. Tada omowaseburi na taido o shiteru dake ja nai ka? ♂
A: That girl looks like she's falling for me.
B: C'mon man. Don't you think she's just teasing you?

A man who deceives women just to get them to have sex with him is an *onnatarashi,* and a man who has only vulgar thoughts on his mind is a *yarashii otoko.*

w: **Yarashii otoko daikirai ya wa.** ♀
e: *Iyarashii otoko daikirai.* ♀
I detest perverted, slimy men.

w: **Mō yarashii koto sentoite.** ♀
e: *Mō iyarashi koto shinaide yo.* ♀
Cut out the sleazy behavior.

Other relevant words include: *chikan* (sleazy man), *chijo* (sleazy woman), *sukebei* (sex fiend), and *hentai* (pervert).

Beautiful People and Nerds

There is a kind of man who does and says things to create a cool image. He has the right things. He knows the right people. But under it all, he's shallow and insincere.

w: **ē kakko shii na hito**
e: *kiza na yatsu*
an affected beautiful person, a show-off

w: **Ano hito ē kakko shii ya ne.**
e: *Ano hito kiza da ne.*
He's a slick show-off.

w: **ē otoko**
e: *ii otoko*
a man with confidence, looks, style

w: **Yappari, ē otoko wa beppin to tsukiaun yaro na.**

e: *Yappa, ii otoko wa bijin to tsukiaun daro.*
It figures, gorgeous men go out with gorgeous women.

w: **Aitsu ikitten ne.** ♂
e: *Aitsu erasō ni shiyagatte.* ♂
He's a cocky SOB, isn't he.

Don't confuse this with *iki na hito,* which has a good meaning.

w: **Ano hito wa sui na hito ya nē.**
e: *Ano hito wa iki na hito da ne.*
She looks really together, confident, stylish, and sexy.

The opposite of an *iki na hito* is a *yabo na hito,* a person with zero style.

w/e: ***Yabo na otoko wa daikirai.***
I loathe nerds.

w/e: ***yabottai***
utterly devoid of taste, boorish, uncouth

w: **inakamon mitai/kakko warui**
e: *dasai*
nerdy

w/e: ***chibi***
a wimpy runt

A girl who looks ugly regardless of her sense of style is called *busu.*

w: **Kanojo busu ya.**
e: *Kanojo (wa) busu da.*
She's a dog.

A fatso is called *debu.*

w: **Kanojo debu ya.**
e: *Kanojo (wa) debu da.*
She's a fat pig.

w: **petanko**
e: *pechanko*
flat

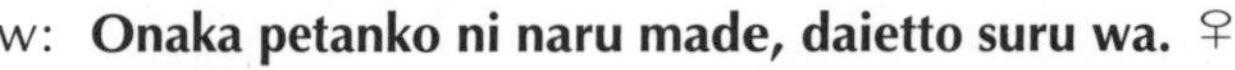

w: **Onaka petanko ni naru made, daietto suru wa.** ♀
e: *Onaka ga pechanko ni naru made, daietto suru wa yo.* ♀
I'm going on a diet until my stomach's flat.

HUGE!

Mecha is constantly used by young people in Western Japan. It sounds like the Spanish *mucho* and has almost the same meaning.

w: **mechamecha/muchamucha/muchakucha/mucha/mecha**
e: *mechakucha*
extremely, totally

w: **Mechamecha kakko ē na.**
e: *Mechakucha kakkō ii ne.*
He's extremely good looking, isn't he?

w: **Metcha ōkii na.**
e: *Sugoku ōkii ne.*
It's huge.

w: **dekai**
e: *ōkii/dekkai*
big, jutting

w: **Aitsu no ketsu dekai.**
e: *Aitsu no ketsu dekkai na.*
He's got a fat ass.

Related words include *deppa* and *dekapai.* The first is a combination of *deru* and *ha* (tooth), and means bucktoothed. The second is a vulgar combination of *dekkai* and *oppai* (breasts), and means big-breasted. *Ano onna mecha dekapai ya de, hora!* is the sort of thing said by teenage boys or slimy *sukebei* men.

THIS STINKS!

In Tōkyō *akan* is considered to be a worse kind of bad than *dame,* and in Kansai *dame* is considered to mean seriously bad and *akan* just means no good or lousy. So unless you are angry or dead serious you should use *akan* in Kansai and *dame* in Kantō. In Hiroshima, *akan* becomes *iken.*

w: **akan**
e: *dame*
bad

In politer speech *akan* is replaced with *akimahen.*

w: **Mō mina akan wa.**
e: *Mō minna dame da wa.*
It stinks in every way.

w: **Akan nen kore wa!/Kora zettai akan nen!**
e: *Kore wa zettai dame da yo!* ♂
This is totally unacceptable./This is awful.

w: **Tabena akan. Ikana akan wa. (Kansai)**
Tabenya iken. Ikanya iken. (Hiroshima)

e: *Tabenakucha. Ikanakucha.*
I have to eat. I have to go.

w: **akantare**
e: *yowamushi*
a spineless person

Another word meaning just about the same as *akantare* is *tako. Ahotare* and *bakatare* mean "jerk" or "idiot" and *kusotare* means "shithead."

w: **waya**
e: *dame*
out of control

w: **Mō waya ya.**
e: *Mō dame da.*
It's already all screwed up.

There is a subtle nuance to *waya* not found in *dame* or *akan,* which is a feeling of despair or disappointment that things have gone wrong.

DUNCES AND SPACE CADETS

Just as *akan* sounds mild in Western Japanese but emphatic in Eastern Japanese, *aho* sounds mild or even jokingly friendly in Western Japanese but emphatically serious in Eastern Japanese. Both *dame* and *baka* sound strong and even insulting in Western Japanese. Be careful!

w: **aho**
e: *baka*
dumb, foolish

w: **Aho chau!**
e: *Baka nan ja nai!*
You dummy!

w: **Ahokusa!**
e: *Bakarashii!*
It's (you're) ridiculous!

w: **Aitsu honma ni aho ya ne.**
e: *Aitsu honto ni baka da ne.*
He's really a jerk.

w: **Aho chaimannen, pā dennen. (Ōsaka, old men's talk)**
e: *Baka ja arimasen, pā nan desu.*
I'm not dumb, I'm foolish.

Pā is a nonsense word meaning "foolish." This sentence is an example of Ōsaka *Naniwa kotoba,* spoken nowadays primarily by older people (see chapter on Ōsaka Style). Young people seem to prefer a more standard Western Japanese or Tōkyō speech depending on how stylish they want to seem. Western Japanese has a familiar feeling to it, whereas those who imitate Tōkyō Japanese may want to present a higher class or *oshare na* image. They imitate Tōkyō Japanese at the risk of being labeled a *kiza* or snobby show-off.

w: **Boke!/Manuke!**
e: *Oboke!*
Imbecile!/You dunce!

Boke derives from *bokeru,* a verb meaning to grow senile. In slang Japanese it is often used to mean muddle-headed. *Manuke* derives from *ma ga nukeru,* which means to be out of tune with what's going on and hence look stupid.

w/e: ***Neboketeru.***
I'm groggy.

w/e: ***nebokegao***
a puffy morning face after having woken up

w: **Bōtto shiterun chau?**
e: *Boketto shiterun ja nai?*
Spacing out?

w: **Bōtto shitotta.**
e: *Boketto shiteta.*
I was spacing out.

w: **Boketara akan!**
e: *Boketto shitcha dame!*
Don't daydream!

w: **bōtto shiteru hito**
e: *bonyari shita hito*
a space cadet, an absent-minded person

w: **shindoi**
e: *tsukareta*
tired, beat

w: **Shindoi wa!**
e: *Tsukarechatta!*
I'm exhausted!

Other words for being tired are *erai* and *taigi. Erai* is heard in Kansai and as far east as Nagoya. *Taigi* is common in and around Hiroshima. Instead of saying *shindoi na,* in Hiroshima they say *taigi ja nō.*

w: **donkusai**
e: *donkusai, guzu*
not too quick, insensitive, boorish, tactless

w: **Anta itsumo donkusai na.**
e: *Anata itsumo donkusai (guzu) da ne.*
Never too quick are you?

w: **Nande sonna donkusain ya?**
e: *Dōshite sonna ni yōryō ga warui no?*
Why are you such a dimwit?

Don't confuse *donkusai* (mentally insensitive) with *donkan* (stolid, physically insensitive) or *donsai* (stupid as in low IQ).

w/e: ***otchokochoi***
spastic, klutzy

A person who always bumps into and spills things can also be described as an *awatembo.*

w: **Watashi awatembo ya.**
e: *Watashi (wa) awatemono na no.*
I'm such a clod.

In Western Japanese, *-bo* is often added to a verb root to indicate a person with the trait of that verb. For example, a person who always forgets appointments and misplaces keys can be called a *wasurembo,* derived from the verb *wasureru* (to forget). A *kikanbo* is a reckless and uncontrollable kid.

In Japan, as elsewhere in the world, it was once considered bad to be left-handed. Thus there is a slightly derogatory undertone to the word *gitcho.*

w: **gitcho**
e: *hidarikiki/gitcho*
left-handed

w: **Eh, anta gitcho ka?**
e: *Eh, anata hidarikiki desu ka?*
What, you're a lefty?

w: **toroi**
e: *noroi*
slow, sluggish

w: **Mada tabeten no?! Toroi na!**
e: *Mada tabeten no?! Noroi na!*
You still eating?! God you're slow!

w: **shinkikusai**
nerve-wrackingly tedious (situation), uptight and boring (person)

w: **Jūtai de shinkikusai na!**
e: *Jūtai de ira tsuku ne!*
It's nerve-wrackingly tedious to be in a traffic jam.

HOW DROLL

If you go to a comedy show with high hopes but it turns out to be utterly asinine and dull, you might utter to yourself *shōmonai* with a sigh and leave. *Shōmonai* has a nuance of resignation or disappointment, as if more had been expected. The *omoshirokunai* of Eastern Japanese does not carry this nuance, nor does *shikata ga nai* (in Western Japanese *shānai*) which means "nothing can be done about it." Compare also *dō shōmo nai,* used in both Eastern and Western Japan, which means something like "I have no idea

what to do" or "I see no way out of this." For example: *Ashita ame ga futtara, dō shōmo nai de* means "If it rains tomorrow we're in real trouble."

w: **shōmonai**
e: *tsumannai/tsumaranai/kudaranai*
pointless, boring, a waste of time

w: **Mata shōmonai koto yan no?**
e: *Mata kudaranai koto yaru no?*
Are you doing something pointless again?

w: **Yappari shōmonakatta na, ano eiga.**
e: *Yappa omoshirokunakatta ne, ano eiga.*
As expected, that movie was a dud.

w: **omoroi**
e: *omoshiroi*
funny, interesting

w: **ē**
e: *ii*
good

w: **Kyō ē o-tenki ya na.**
e: *Kyō wa ii o-tenki da ne.*
Beautiful weather today, huh.

w: **Kore de ēn chau?**
e: *Kore de ii jan?/Kore de iin ja nai?*
This is good enough, don't you think?

Jan? is a derivative of *ja nai?* and is very popular with young people in Eastern Japan. The Western Japanese version is *chau?* derived from *chigau?* It means "right?" or "don't you think so?"

OLD AND YOUNG

Back home, if you're naive you're said to be green. But in Japan your bottom is blue!

w: **Anta mada ketsu ga aoi yanka.**
e: *Anata 'tte mada kodomo ne.*
You're still green.

w: **aoi**
e: *wakai*
green, young

This usage of *aoi* (blue) may derive from the fact that Japanese babies are born with a blue spot on their rumps called *mōkohan* (Mongolian mark), which disappears after a few months.

w: **otchan /ossan**
e: *ojisan*
(old) man

w: **Ossan nonde bakkari shitetara akan de.**
e: *Ojisan nonde bakari shitcha dame yo.*
Hey old man, it's no good if all you do is drink.

Ossan is not a particularly polite word and can be used either derogatorily or jokingly in Western Japan. Related words are *obahan* (auntie), *babā* (crabby old lady), *jijii* (crabby old man), and the now popular *obatarian* (a tough, pushy battle-axe).

w: **gochagocha yū**
e: *gujiguji iu*
to nag

w: **Nani gocha gocha yūton nen, anta, mō ē yan?**
e: *Nani gujiguji itten no, anata, mō ii ja nai?*
What are you nagging for? It's enough already.

In contrast, *butsubutsu iu* means "to complain mumblingly to oneself," and *guchagucha* means "soggy" or "mushy."

8

KANSAI GRAMMAR AND SPECIAL EXPRESSIONS

In addition to the main differences between Western and Eastern Japanese summarized in the seven points at the beginning of this book, there are many finer distinctions between the two that will be looked at here.

KANSAI GRAMMAR

Abbreviations and Contractions

There are many abbreviations used in Japanese that make speech, especially tough male speech, all but unintelligible to foreigners unless they have specifically studied them. The following is a basic list of the most common substitutions and elisions in Japanese. Instances where the change pertains only to Western Japanese are marked.

are wa → arya
Are wa nani darō? → Arya nan darō?
What on earth is that?

arimasen, nai → arya shinai (emphatic, from ari wa shinai)
Chokin wa arimasen. → Chokin wa arya shinai.
I have no savings.

chigaimasu → chaimasu (Western)

Zenzen chigaimasu yo! → *Zenzen chaimasu yo!*
That's totally wrong!

chigau → chau (Western)
to be wrong

chotto → chō, choi
Chotto matte!→*Chō matte!*
Wait a second!

da → ya, ja (Western)

de mo → datte (-te mo → -tatte)

desu → -su
Sō desu ne. → *Sōsu ne.*
You're right.

de wa → ja
De wa mata. → *Ja mata.*
See you later.

doko ka → dokka
somewhere

ii → ē (Western)
Ii yo! → *ē wa!*
Fine!

iru → oru (Western)
to be (animals and people)

iu → yū (Western)
to say

ka? → kai?, dai? (men's question particles)
Taberu ka? → *Taberu kai?*
Do you want to eat?
Kore nan da? → *Kore nan dai?*
What is this?

-ko kara → -kkara
Asoko kara . . . → *Asokkara . . .*
From there . . .

kore wa → korya, kora
Kore wa mechakucha yo. → *Korya mechakucha yo.*

This is really terrible.

mono → mon

Kaimono ni itta. → *Kaimon ni itta.*

He went shopping.

moratta → morōta (Western)

received

na no → nan

Sō na no. → *Sō nan da.*

That's true.

-nai → -n, -hen (Western)

-nakereba → -nakucha, -nakya (Eastern)

Ganbaranakucha.

You have to go for it.

-nakereba → -na, -nya (Western)

Ganbarana akan

You have to go for it.

nanika → nanka

Nanika hoshii? → *Nanka hoshii?*

Would you like something?

nantonaku → nanka

Nantonaku Amerika e ikitai wa. → *Nanka Amerika e ikitai wa.*

I'm not sure why, but I feel like going to America.

ni wa → nya

Boku ni wa iwanai hō ga ii yo. → *Boku nya iwanai hō ga ii yo.*

It would be better if you didn't tell me.

no → -n

Mō itta no da. → *Mō ittan da.*

She already went.

no de → -nde

Tabemasu no de . . . → *Tabemasunde . . .*

Because we will eat . . .

-reba → -rya (Eastern)

Itte kureba ii no ni. → *Itte kurya ii no ni.*

It would be good if he went for us.

Benkyō sureba gōkaku dekiru darō. → *Benkyō surya gōkaku dekiru darō.*
If you study you can probably pass.

-ru → -n

Nani yatteru no? → *Nani yatten no?*
What are you doing?
O-kane aru nen yanka. → *O-kane an nen yanka.*
Look, I have money.
Ashita kuru nen yanka. → *Ashita kun nen yanka.*
He's coming tomorrow.

sore wa → sorya, sora

Sore wa sō da. → *Sora sō da.*
That's right.

-ta darō → -tarō

Mō itta darō. → *Mō ittarō.*
He probably left already.

-te ageru (-te yaru) → -taru (Western)

Shashin totte ageyō ka? → *Shashin tottarō ka?*
Shall I take a picture for you?

-te ageta → -tatta (Western)

Yatte ageta. → *Yattatta.*
I did it for him.

-te arimasu → -taru, -teru

Messēji ga kaite aru. → *Messēji ga kaitaru.*
A message is written down.

-te inai → -tenai, -te ya shinai (emphatic)

Mada nete inai. → *Mada netenai.*
He's not sleeping yet.
Hyaku-en shika motte inai. → *Hyaku-en shika motte hen.* (Western)
I only have a hundred yen.

-te iru → -teru, -ten

Nani yatteru no? → *Nani yatten no?*
What are you doing?

-te ita → -teta

Kyō ichinichijū nete ita. → *Kyō ichinichijū neteta.*

I slept all day today.

-te ite → -tete

-te miro! → -te mi! -te mii! (Western)

Kotchi kite miro! → *Kotchi kite mii!*

Just try coming over here!

-te oku → -toku

Yamete okō. → *Yametokō.*

Let's not do it (something we had planned to do).

-te iru → -toru, -ton (Western)

Nani mite iru no? → *Nani miton no?*

What are you looking at?

-te ita → -totta, -totten (Western)

Kangaegoto shite ita. → *Kangaegoto shitotta.*

I was lost in thought.

-te shimatta → -te shimōta, -te mōta (Western)

Kasa wasurete shimatta. → *Kasa wasurete mōta.*

I forgot my umbrella.

-te shimatta → -chatta, -jatta (Eastern)

Itte shimatta. → *Itchatta.*

He left.

Shinde shimatta. → *Shinjatta.*

He died.

-te shimau → -chau (Eastern), -chimau (Eastern, men)

Basu ga itte shimau. → *Basu ga itchau.*

The bus is going.

-te shimau → -te mau (Western).

Basu ga itte shimau. → *Basu ga itte mau.*

The bus is going.

-te wa → -cha

Tabete wa dame. → *Tabecha dame.* (Eastern)

You must not eat.

to → te, 'te

"Hello" *to itta.* → "Hello" *'te itta.*
He said "hello."

tokoro → toko
place

CONDITIONALS

Future Conditional

In conversational Western Japanese, the most common conditional pattern is *moshi . . . tara . . . . Moshi* is used to emphasize the conditionality of a sentence, but is not essential.

w: **Ashita akankattara ikahen yaro.**
e: *Ashita dame dattara* (or *nara) ikanai daro.*
If it's bad tomorrow, (he) probably won't go.

w: **Moshi wakarahenkattara setsumei shitaro ka?**
Moshi wakarahen nen yattara setsumei shitaro ka?
e: *Moshi wakaranakattara setsumei shite ageyō ka?*
If you don't understand, shall I explain it to you?

Subjunctive

w: **Moshi watashi ga kaseijin yattara toberu yarō.**
e: *Moshi watashi ga kaseijin nara toberu darō.*
If I were a Martian I could fly.

w: **Nihonjin yattara ē no ni.**
e: *Nihonjin dattara ii no ni.*
I wish I were Japanese.

w: **Kinō doku o nonda to shitara, mō shinderu hazu ya.**

Kinō doku o nondan yattara, mō shinderu hazu ya.

e: *Kinō doku o nonda to shitara, mō shinderu hazu da.*
Assuming he drank poison yesterday, he should be dead already.

Past Conditional

In standard Japanese there are many ways to express the past conditional tense using *-ta/da +ra, nara, naraba,* and *-eba.* The expression most commonly used in conversation, *ta/da+ra,* will be considered here.

w: **Ano hikōki ni nottetara, shinde ita yarō na.**
e: *Ano hikōki ni nottetara, shinde ita darō na.*
If you had taken that plane, you would have been dead.

w: **Moshi kinō no kotoba ga warukattan yattara, ayamaru wa.**
e: *Moshi kinō no kotoba ga warukattan dattara, ayamaru yo.*
If what I said yesterday was bad, I apologize.

Conditional sentences that end in . . . *no ni* convey a sense of regret.

w: **Mō chotto yasukattara kōta no ni nā.**
e: *Mō chotto yasukattara, katta no ni nā.*
If it had been a little bit cheaper, I would have bought it.

w: **Moshi hikōki no chiketto ga torehen 'te wakatten yattara shinkansen de itta no ni.**
e: *Moshi hikōki no chiketto ga torenai to wakatte itara shinkansen de itta no ni.*
If I'd realized I couldn't get a plane ticket, I'd have gone by bullet train.

-na akan

The phrase for "must" in Eastern Japanese follows the pattern verb root +*nakereba narimasen.* In Western Japanese the most common pattern is verb root +*na akan. Akan* is an abbreviation of *akimahen* meaning "bad" or "lousy."

w: **Hayō ikana akan wa.**
Hayō ikanya akan nen.
Hayō ikenya iken. (Hiroshima)
e: *Hayaku ikanakereba naranai.*
Hayaku ikanakya.
Hayaku ikanakya ikenai.
Hayaku ikanakucha.
I have to go right away.

w: **Ganbarana akan wa.**
e: *Ganbaranakucha.*
You've got to go for it.

Another less common way to say "must" uses . . . *to akan.*

w: **Motto benkyō sento akan nen.**
Motto benkyō sena akan wa.
e: *Motto benkyō shinai to dame da.*
Motto benkyō shinakya.
I have to study more.

The next pattern derives from a more general usage of *to* (if).

w: **Yappari tabena, hara heru yarō.** ♂
Yappari taben to onaka suku yarō.
e: *Yappari tabenai to hara heru yo.* ♂
Yappari tabenai to onaka suku yo.
You know, if you don't eat you're going to get hungry.

-shite

There is a tendency in Western Japan to replace the *se* in verbs like *miseru* (to show), *noseru* (to load on), *saseru* (to make do), and *motaseru* (to let have, to have carry), with *shi* in the past tense and *-te* form.

w: **Mishite chōdai.**
e: *Misete kudasai.*
Let me have a look.

w: **Noshite kurete arigatō.**
e: *Nosete kurete arigatō.*
Thanks for giving me a lift.

w: **Tabesashita.**
e: *Tabesaseta.*
I made (them) eat./I let (them) eat.

-te

When speaking informally, a *te* is added to the end of sentences to convey the meanings "I heard that," "He said that," or "They say that." In colloquial Eastern Japanese, the ending is a crisper *tte*. The endings *te* or *tte* are the abbreviations of *to kiita, to kiita koto ga aru,* or *to iimashita.*

w: **Mada are o motte kaette kurehen nente.**
e: *Mada are o motte kaette kurenain datte.*
It seems he hasn't brought it back yet.

Sentences ending in . . . *tente* are frequently used one after the other when narrating a series of events that have happened. The following is a typical example of immature male locker room gossip in Japan.

w: **Kinō na, Wataru nā, ē onna ni ōtente. Honde na, nanpa shitente. Shinjirarehen wa! Nanka, rabu-hoteru ni itte!**
e: *Kinō sa, Wataru sā, ii onna ni attan da 'tte. De sa, nanpa shitan datte. Shinjiran nē yo. De, rabu-hoteru ni itte sa!*
Yesterday, right, Wataru met this great chick. And then he did her. I can't believe it! They went to a love hotel or something.

-ten, -ton

The verb endings *-ten* and *-ton,* in order of decreasing politeness, are Western Japanese abbreviations for the standard *-te iru* or *-teru* endings.

w: **Ware nani yatton (miton, yūton) ja kora! (♂ vulgar)**
e: *Temē nani yatten (miten, itten) da kora! (♂ very vulgar)*
What the hell do you think you're doing (looking at, saying)!

w: **Nani yatton nen?** ♂
Nani yatten nen?
e: *Nani yatteru no?*
What are you doing?

w: **Okonomiyaki tabeten ya de.** ♂
Okonomiyaki tabeten nen.
e: *Okonomiyaki o tabeterun desu yo.*
Okonomiyaki tabeteru yo.
I'm eating okonomiyaki.

w: **Kyō mina wasureton chau?**
e: *Kyō minna wasureterun ja nai?*
Looks like everybody's forgetting something today, don't you think?

w: **Ano ko ga naiton ya wa./Ano ko naiten nen.**
e: *Ano ko ga naiteru.*
He's crying.

w: **Akachan ga naitō noni, dare mo ayashite kurehen nen. (Kōbe)**
e: *Akachan ga naiteru noni, dare mo ayashite kuremasen.*
Even though the baby's crying, nobody's comforting him.

-teta, -totta

The verb endings *-totta, -totten, -yotta,* and *-tetan* are Western Japanese abbreviations for the Eastern *-te imashita* or *-teta* endings. Remember that *iru* in Western Japanese is *oru.* Thus the Eastern Japanese *tabete ita* becomes *tabete ota* or *tabetotta.*

w: **Sakki nani hanashitotten?** ♂
Sakki nani hanashitetan? ♀
e: *Sakki nani hanashite ita?*
Sakki nani hanashiteta no? ♂
What were you just talking about?
What've you been talking about?

w: **Nani yattotten?** ♂
Nani yattetan? ♀
e: *Nani yattetan dai?* ♂
Nani yatte ita no?/Nani yatteta no?
What've you been doing?

w: **Pūru ni haittottan chau?** ♂
Pūru ni haittetan chau? ♀
e: *Pūru ni haitte itan ja nai?*
Pūru ni haitteta jan?
Wasn't she in the pool?

w: **Shimōta, kagi wasurettoten ya.** ♂
Shimōtta, kagi wasuretetan ya wa. ♀
e: *Shimatta, kagi wasuretan da yo.* ♂
Shimatta, kagi wasureta no yo. ♀
Damn, I forgot the key.

w: **Kyō nani shitotta?**
e: *Kyō nani shiteta?*
What did you do today?

w: **Mō ichi-jikan gurai benkyō shitotta.**
e: *Mō ichi-jikan gurai benkyō shiteta.*
He's already studied about an hour.

w: **Tegami kakiyotta. / Denwa kakeyotta. / Kakeochi shiyotta. (Kōbe)**
e: *Tegami kaiteta. /Denwa kaketeta. / Kakeochi shiteta.*
He wrote. / He called. / He eloped.

Note that the *-yotta* ending cannot be used to refer to one's own actions.

-toite

In Eastern Japan women generally say *iwanaide kudasai* when they want you not to say something. In Western Japan women tend to use the somewhat stronger *iwantoite.* It is not uncommon for men to use the tough *iu na* in both Eastern and Western Japan. The *-toite* ending derives from *-te oku:* to do something and keep doing it.

w: **Sunentoite.** ♀
e: *Sunenaide.*
Don't pout.

w: **Kore tabentoite na.** ♀
e: *Kore o tabenaide kudasai.*
Please don't eat this.

w: **Koko de kane hirogentoite ya.**
e: *Koko de o-kane o hirogenaide.*
Don't spread the money out here.

This might be said by a clerk to a small boy who dumps a bunch of coins on the counter at a supermarket.

w: **Atashi no koto o baka ni sentoite.**
e: *Atashi no koto o baka ni shinaide.*
Don't make fun of me.

w: **Miantoite!**
e: *Minaide!*
Don't look!

SPECIAL KANSAI EXPRESSIONS

Ageru Abbreviated

There are some special abbreviations in Western Japanese that can be used in place of the verb + *ageru* forms, which signal an action being done for someone else. They are actually abbreviations of -*te yaru* as opposed to *-te ageru,* and therefore should definitely not be used when talking to superiors.

w: **Shashin tottarō ka?**
e: *Shashin o totte ageyō ka?*
Shall I take a picture (of you)?

w: **Omae o tsurete ittaro ka?**
e: *Kimi o tsurete itte ageyō ka?*
Shall I take you?

The *-te ageta* form becomes *-tatta* as follows.

w: **Kanojo no tame ni pātii o shitatta.**
e: *Kanojo no tame ni pātii o shite ageta.*
We had a party for her.

w: **Kippu o kōtatta noni, itte kurehenkatta.**
e: *Kippu o katte ageta noni, itte kurenakatta.*
Even though I bought a ticket for her, she didn't go.

Similarly, *ogotte ageta* (treated to) becomes *ogottatta, yatte ageta* (did for) becomes *yattatta,* and *tsukutte ageta* (made for) becomes *tsukuttatta.*

w: **Hiro-san no taiya o mitatte ne.**
e: *Hiro-san no taiya o mite agete ne.*
Look at Hiro's tire for him, will you?

Chau

Chau is an abbreviation of *chigau* (different or not right). In Western Japanese it is used in the same way as *ja nai* or *jan.*

w: **Aho chau.**
e: *Baka ja nai.*
You dummy.

w: **Chaun chau (ka).**
e: *Chigaun ja nai?*
That's wrong, right?

w: **Jōdan chau de!**
e: *Jōdan ja nē yo!*
Stop joking!

w: **Chau de!**
e: *Dame yo!*
No way!/That's wrong!

w: **Aitsu shigoto yameyottan chau?** ♂
e: *Aitsu shigoto yametan ja nai?* ♂
He quit work, right?

Compare the differences in the following translations for "that's completely wrong." *Zenzen chau wa* is said when one is talking to oneself, similar to the way people say "no, wait" after realizing they made a mistake. *Zenzen chau no* can be a statement or a question, depending on the speaker's intonation. *Zenzen chau de* is emphatic.

De

Tacked onto the end of a sentence for emphasis, *de* means "I'm telling you." It is used instead of *ze* or *yo*.

w: **Mō san-ji ya de!**
e: *Mō san-ji da yo!*
Hey, it's already 3 o'clock!

De is used in this way much more in Western than in Eastern Japan.

Donai

In colloquial Western Japanese, *dō* (how) changes to *donai*. However, in young people's talk, *dō* is used more than *donai*.

w: **Saikin donai shitotten? ♂/Saikin donai shitetan? ♀**
e: *Saikin dō shiteta?*
How've you been doing lately?

w: **Dō shitan?/Donai shitan?**
e: *Dō shita?*
What's the matter? / What's going on?

w: **Aitsu donai shiten nen. ♂/Ano ko dō shiten no? ♀**
e: *Aitsu dō shiteru? ♂/Ano ko dō shiteru? ♀*
How's he doing?

w; **Donai ya?**
e: *Dō?*
How about it?

E

E is used in Western Japan in place of *yo*. It adds emphasis to a sentence.

w: **Honma ni omoroi desse! (Ōsaka)**
e: *Honto ni omoshiroi desu yo!*
It's really funny!

Honde, Honara

In Western Japanese the *"s"* sound is often replaced with an *"h."* For example, *ikimasen* becomes *ikimahen, soshite* becomes *honde,* and *soshitara* becomes *honara* or, in Ōsaka, *hondara*. The exact origin of this trend is unknown, but some speculate that it developed in Western Japan from the lisping speech of ancient Kyōto aristocracy.

w: **Honnara (honara) iko ka?/Hondara iko ka? (Ōsaka ♂)**
e: *Soshitara ikō ka?*
O.K. Let's go.

w: **Kare ni kirai to yuwareten. Hondemo akiramerarehen nen.**
e: *Kare ni kirai to iwareta no. Dakedo akiramerarenai wa.*
He said he doesn't like me. But I can't give up.

w: **Ashi arahenkatten ya. Honde na, zutto aruite kaette mōtan ya.**
e: *Kuruma ga nakattan da. Sore de sa, zutto aruite kaechatta no yo.*
I didn't have a car. So I walked the whole way back.

Honde is often pronounced with so little stress on *ho* that it sounds like *-nde*. A sentence can also begin with *De . . .* (And so).

Ja nashi ni/ Ya nōte

Ja nashi ni and *ya nōte* negate what goes before them, and generally precede a counter claim. For example:

w: **Amerika e ittan ya nōte, Kanada e ittan chau?**
e: *Amerika e ittan ja nakute, Kanada e ittan ja nai no?*
He didn't go to America. He went to Canada, right?

w:**A: Koitsu! Nusunda yarō.**
B: Sō ya nōte! Nusundan to chau de! Kōte mōtan ya de!
e: *A: Koitsu! Nusunda darō.*
B: Sō ja nai! Nusundan ja nai ze! Katte morattan da yo!
A: You little rat! You stole it!
B: No way! I didn't steal it! Somebody bought it for me!

w: **Kore ya nōte, are ya wa.**
e: *Kore ja nakute, are desu.*
It's not this. It's that.

w: **Ippen no yasumi mo nashi de, zutto hataraiteten.**
e: *Ikkai no yasumi mo nakute, zutto hataraitetan da.*
Without a single vacation, he worked the whole time.

w: **Kankei nashi.**
e: *Kankei nai.*
That's irrelevant./It doesn't matter.

Kaina

A sentence ending in *-kaina* means "It can't be that" or "There's no way it's that."

w: **Aitsu ni ā iu keiken aru kaina.**
e: *Aitsu ni ā iu keiken ga aru hazu (wa) nai.*
There's no way he's had that sort of experience.

w: **Honma kaina!**
e: *Jōdan ja nē yo!* ♂/ *Uso bakkari!*
You've gotta be kidding./Get out of here!

w: **Ano hito (wa) otoko kaina. Nanka onna mitai.**
e: *Ano hito (wa) otoko na no? Nanka onna mitai.* ♀
Aitsu otoko ka yo. Nanka onna mitai. ♂
He can't be a man. He looks like a woman or something.

Kate

In Eastern Japan *keredomo* is abbreviated *keredo* or the familiar sounding *kedo*. In Western Japan, both *kedo* and *kate* are used.

w: **Sonna koto yūta kate, sugu (ni) wa dekihin wa.**
e: *Sonna koto o itta kedo, sugu (ni) wa dekimasen.*
Even though he said so, we can't finish it immediately.

w: **Tanaka-san no uchi itta kate, rusu ya de.**
e: *Tanaka-san no uchi ni ittemo, rusu da yo.*
I went to Tanaka's house, but he wasn't in.

w: **Denwa shita kate, dare mo dēhenkattan.**
e: *Denwa shita kedo, dare mo denakatta yo.*
I called, but nobody answered.

Mitai

In colloquial Western or Eastern Japanese, it is far more common to hear a sentence meaning "It seems that . . ." end in *mitai* than in *rashii. Rashii* sounds more learned or authoritative. *Mitai* at the end of a sentence also means "looks like."

w:**A: Anta marude shitsuren shita mitai ya wa. Nanka attan ka?**
B: Mm, sō ya nen, senshū furareta.
e: *A: Anata marude shitsuren shita mitai. Nanika atta no?*
B: Mm, datte, senshū furareta wake.
A: You look like you're heartbroken. Is something wrong?
B: Yeah, well, last week I was dumped (by my boyfriend).

w: **Sensei wa mō dekakehatta mitai.**
e: *Sensei wa mō o-dekake ni natta mitai.*
Looks like the teacher already left.

Morōta

Morōta or *mōta* is often used for *moratta* in Western Japan.

w: **Sanpatsu shite morōtan ya.**
e: *Tokoya ni ittan da.*
I got a haircut.

Note that *kōte mōta* can mean either *katte moratta* (I had someone buy it for me) or *katte shimatta* (I bought it). *Morōta* is actually more correct, but when people speak quickly it sometimes get slurred into *mōta*.

Na 1

This use of *na* means "Isn't it so?" It is a Western Japanese substitute for *ne*.

w: **Kanojo kirei ya na.**
e: *Kanojo (wa) kirei da ne.*
She's pretty, isn't she.

w: **Asoko kirekatta na.**
e: *Asoko wa kirei datta ne.*
That place was pretty, wasn't it.

In Kansai, women also use this particle. But if a woman were to finish her sentences with *na* in Kantō, she'd probably be considered vulgar.

Na 2

Another use of *na* means "I wonder" in both Western and Eastern Japanese.

w: **Amerika e ikarehen ka na.**
e: *Amerika e ikenai ka na.*
I wonder if I won't be able to go to America.

Na 3

This *na* is used in Western Japan instead of *sa*. It makes sure that one's listener is indeed listening.

w: **Kinō na, ore wa na, oyaji to issho ni tsuri shitottan ya de.**
e: *Kinō sa, ore sa, oyaji to issho ni tsuru shitetan da yo.*
Yesterday, right, I went fishing with my old man.

Na 3 is the most common usage of *na* in Western Japan.

Nā 1

Nā can be used instead of *na* or *nē* as an exclamation.

w: **Ame ga yō furimasu nā!**
e: *Ame ga yoku furimasu nē!*
Wow, it's sure raining hard! (Also used by women in Western Japan.)

Nā 2

This *nā* asks the listener to agree with something. For a similar effect in Eastern Japan, *nē* is generally used.

w: **Kirei ya nā.**
e: *Kirei da nē.*
It's pretty, don't you think?

Na (na 1) and *nā* (nā 2), as in *Ē o-tenki ya na!* and *Ē o-tenki ya nā!* have slightly different nuances. The first makes a statement, "Sure is good weather!" and would likely evoke a response like "Mm," meaning "Sure is." The second is more of an explicit request for concurrence: "Great weather, don't you think?" and would likely evoke an agreement, such as *Ē, honma ni kirei ya na.*

Nā 3

Another use of *nā* indicates a wish.

w: **Kane ga areba ē nā.**
e: *Okane ga areba ii nā.*
I wish I had money.

Ne and *nē* are used in the same way as *na* and *nā,* but have a softer, more polite tone.

Nen

Nen is used in Western Japan to show familiarity.

w: **Kōtemo kamahen nen.**
e: *Kattemo kamawanai.*
I don't care if he bought it.

w: **Sore de ē nen.**
e: *Sore de iin da.*
It's good that way.

w: **Watashi mō shitten nen yo.**
e: *Watashi mō shitteru no yo.* ♀
Watashi mō shitterun yo. ♂
Look, I already know.

w: **Sō ya kedo ichiban yarashi toko nuketen nen.**
e: *Demo ichiban iyarashi tokoro wa nuketerun da.*
But the most sexually explicit part's left out.

w: **Denwa sento akan de.**
e: *Denwa shinai to dame da yo.*
You must call.

w: **Mō ē nen.**
e: *Mō ii.*
Enough already.

Neyan

Neyan is used in Western Japan to show familiarity. It has basically the same meaning as *nen.*

w: **Nani yūten neyan?**
e: *Nani itten no?*
What do you think you're saying?

w: **Nani kangaeten neyan?**
e: *Nani kangaeten no?*
What are you thinking?

Other forms of *neyan* include *neya* and *nya.*

Nō

Nō is the male form of *na* or *ne.*

w: **Kirei ya nō.**
Kirei ja nō (Hiroshima)
e: *Kirei desu ne.*
It's pretty, don't you think?

Shimōta

In Eastern Japanese *tabeta* means "I ate" and *tabete shimatta* means "I ate it up" or "I ate and am done." That is, adding *shimatta or shimaimashita* to the *-te* form of a verb generally emphasizes the completion of the action. In Western Japanese, *shimatta* becomes *shimōta* or *mōta,* the latter being used primarily by men.

w: **Jitensha kōte shimōta./Jitensha kōte mōta.**
e: *Jitensha o katte shimatta./Jitensha katchatta.*
I bought a bike.

w: **Shimōta! Kagi wasurete kita.**
e: *Shimatta! Kagi wasurete kita.*
Damn! I forgot to bring the key.

w: **Senshū shinde mōtan ya nen./Senshū shinde mōta.**
e: *Senshū shinjatta.*
(He) died last week.

Wa

Wa adds assertion in Western Japanese and is used by both men and women. In Eastern Japan it is used mainly by females.

w: **Mō chō matana akan wa.**
e: *Mō chotto matanakya naranai yo.*
I've got to keep waiting a bit longer.

w: **Doko ni oru ka shiran wa.**
e: *Doko ni iru ka shiranain da yo.* ♂
I don't know where he is.

w: **Ganbarana akan wa!**
e: *Ganbaranakucha!*
You've got to go for it!

Yanka

The word *yanka,* or the tougher sounding men's *yanke,* is used at the end of a phrase or sentence and is very common in Western Japanese. It has no exact equivalent in Eastern Japanese, but its closest equivalent is probably *darō* or *ja nai ka?* It can convey nuances of irritation, indignation, boastfulness, or friendliness, depending on how it is used.

w: **Atarimae yanka!**
e: *Atarimae darō!*
C'mon, it's obvious!

w: **Mada tabeten yanka!**
e: *Mada tabeterun da yo!*
Hey, I'm still eating!

This might be said to someone who is reaching to clear the plates away.

w: **Aitsu no atama marude panku yanke. Mohikan chau?** ♂
e: *Aitsu no atama (wa) marude panku no yō da. Mohikan ja nē ka?* ♂
His hair's just like a punk rocker's. That's a mohawk right?

Much as *sa* is used as a lively, youthful sentence breaker in Tōkyō slang, *yanka* is used as a sentence breaker in Kansai slang.

w: **Kinō na, Mayumi-chan ga otten yanke. Nanka na, muchakucha bikkuri shiten yanke. Honde na, ore ni hanashikaketen yanke. Shinjirarehenkatta, honma ni. Nanka, konban wa te yuwarete, zenzen kotaerarehenkatta wa.**
e: *Kinō sa, Mayumi-chan ga itan da yo. Nanka mechakucha odoroichatte sa. Sore kara, ore ni hanashikaketan da yo. Shinjirarenakatta yo, hontō ni. Nanka, konban wa te iwarete sa, zenzen kotaerarenakatta ze.*
Yesterday, right, Mayumi was, like, there, you know? I was like totally surprised. And then she came up and

talked to me. It was like, I couldn't believe it. Really. She says like good evening, right? And I, like, I couldn't answer at all.

Yanka, like *nanka,* often acts as near meaningless filler, much as "you know" or "like" does in American English.

w: **Amerika no ichiban ōkina shū? Eto na, are yanka, ano nante yūtan yatta'kke? Arasuka yarō. Mm, Arasuka ya de. Mm, honma ni.**
e: *Amerika no ichiban ōkina shū? Eto ne, ma, are darō, ano nan to iun dakke? Arasuka darō. Mm, Arasuka da yo. Mm, kitto.*
America's biggest state? Um, it's that uh, that what do you call it? Alaska, I think. Yeah, it's Alaska. For sure.

w:**A: Kono uta utōten no wa dare ya to omou?**
B: Eto, ano kashu yarō. Are yanka. Madonna yarō.
e: *A: Kono uta o utatteru no wa dare da to omou?*
B: Eto, ano kashu darō. Nan dakke. Madonna darō.
A: Who do you think's singing this song?
B: Uh, that singer, what's her name? Madonna I think.

Are yarō and *are ya wa* have pretty much the same meaning as *are yanka.*

Yo

Yo is used for emphasis in both Western and Eastern Japanese.

w: **Mō deta yo.**
e: *Mō deta yo./Mō dechattan da yo.* ♂
He left already.

Ze

Ze is used by men to mean an emphatic "I'm telling you!" mainly in Eastern Japanese.

w: **Yattā!**
e: *Yatta ze!*
I did it!

Zo

Zo is used mainly by men to add emphasis in both Western and Eastern Japanese.

w: **Hayō hashiru zo!**
e: *Hayaku hashiru zo!*
Let's run fast!

w: Kimi wa kubi ya zo! ♂
e: *Kimi wa kubi da zo!* ♂
You're fired!

Other Titles in the Tuttle Language Library

COMPLETE JAPANESE EXPRESSION GUIDE by *Mizue Sasaki*

> "Studying Japanese idiomatic expressions doesn't have to be a futile exercise in *hitori-zumo* (one man sumo) any longer." —*The Japan Times*

THE COMPLETE JAPANESE VERB GUIDE *compiled by the Hiroo Japanese Center*

> ". . . a real charmer for people who want to liven up their Japanese." —*The Nippon View*

EVEN MONKEYS FALL FROM TREES AND OTHER JAPANESE PROVERBS *by David Galef*

> "This is a likeable book and it tells us much about Japan." —*Edward G. Seidensticker*

A GUIDE TO LEARNING HIRAGANA & KATAKANA *by Kenneth G. Henshall withTetsuo Takagaki*

> ". . . An eminently useful text for the student who wishes to master the two Japanese syllabaries of hiragana and katakana." —*The Daily Yomiuri*

A GUIDE TO READING & WRITING JAPANESE *edited by Florence Sakade*

"Invaluable to anyone eager to acquaint himself with an elementary knowledge of written Japanese."—*Asian Student*

A GUIDE TO REMEMBERING JAPANESE CHARACTERS *by Kenneth G. Henshall*

"Highly recommended . . ." —*Tokyo Journal*

JAPANESE FOR ALL OCCASIONS *by Anne Kaneko*

". . . a godsend to all non-native speakers." —*Nikkei Weekly*

KANJI POWER *by JohnMillen*

"Clear, straightforward, and easy to use. The definitive tool for kanji beginners."
—*Mizue Sasaki, columnist, Asahi Evening News*

MARTIN'S POCKET DICTIONARY *by Samuel E. Martin*

"This is a boon for those of us who may speak Japanese but never properly learned to read or write kanji."

—Donald Richie, The Japan Times

THE MODERN READER'S JAPANESE-ENGLISH CHARACTER DICTIONARY (2nd Revised Edition) *by Andrew N. Nelson*

"This new compilation offers many advantages: a larger number of characters . . ., more readings still in current use . . ., and a greatly expanded listing of compounds . . ."

—Harvard Journal of Asiatic Studies

A REFERENCE GRAMMAR OF JAPANESE *by Samuel E. Martin*

"This grammar . . . is by far the most comprehensive reference grammar of Japanese in the English language (and perhaps in any language)."

—Journal of Linguistics

SPEAK JAPANESE TODAY *by Takeo Kamiya*

"An ideal text for busy people who want to learn Japanese quickly."

—Hiroo Japanese Center